A TREASURY OF
MEMORABLE QUOTATIONS

A Treasury of

MEMORABLE
QUOTATIONS

◆ **B O O K** ◆ **B L O C K S** ◆

Contents

❦   He wrapped himself in quotations –
as a beggar would enfold himself in
the purple of emperors.

Rudyard Kipling

A Gamble at
Terrible Odds

❧ Life is a gamble at terrible odds – if it was a bet, you wouldn't take it.

Tom Stoppard 1937—
British playwright

❧ What a queer thing Life is! So unlike anything else, don't you know, if you see what I mean.

P. G. Wodehouse 1881–1975
English writer

❧ Life is not a series of gig lamps symmetrically arranged; life is a luminous halo, a semi-transparent envelope surrounding us from the beginning of consciousness to the end.

Virginia Woolf 1882–1941
English novelist

❦ There is much good luck in the world, but it is luck. We are none of us safe. We are children, playing or quarrelling on the line.

E. M. Forster 1879–1970
English novelist

❦ I have always maintained that whether a black cat crossing your path is lucky or unlucky depends on whether you are a man or a mouse.

Bernard Levin 1928—
English journalist and author

❦ We can't all be happy, we can't all be rich, we can't all be lucky – and it would be so much less fun if we were . . . Some must cry so that others may be able to laugh the more heartily.

Jean Rhys *c.* 1890–1979
British novelist and short-story writer

❧ We shall generally find that the triangular person has got into the square hole, the oblong into the triangular, and a square person has squeezed himself into the round hole. The officer and the office, the doer and the thing done, seldom fit so exactly that we can say they were almost made for each other.

Sydney Smith 1771–1845
English clergyman and essayist

❧ We have the highest authority for believing that the meek shall inherit the earth; though I have never found any particular corroboration of this aphorism in the records of Somerset House.

F. E. Smith 1872–1930
British Conservative politician and lawyer

❧ Perhaps the rare and simple pleasure of being
   seen for what one is compensates for the
   misery of being it.

Margaret Drabble 1939—
English novelist

❧ True guilt is guilt at the obligation one owes
   to oneself to be oneself. False guilt is guilt
   felt at not being what other people feel one
   ought to be or assume that one is.

R. D. Laing 1927–89
Scottish psychiatrist

❧ So much of life [is] a putting-off of
   unhappiness for another time. Nothing
   [is] ever lost by delay.

Graham Greene 1904–91
English novelist

❧ Affluence was, quite simply, a question of
texture . . . The threadbare carpets of infancy,
the coconut matting, the ill-laid linoleum, the
utility furniture . . . had all spoken of a life too
near the bones of subsistence, too little padded,
too severely worn.

Margaret Drabble 1939—
English novelist

❧ Life is first boredom, then fear.
Whether or not we use it, it goes,
And leaves what something hidden from
                                        us chose,
And age, and then the only end of age.

Philip Larkin 1922–85
English poet

❦ Is there no way out of the mind?

Sylvia Plath 1932–63
American poet

❦ We're all of us sentenced to solitary
   confinement inside our own skins, for life!

Tennessee Williams 1911–83
American playwright

❦ The secret of being miserable is to have leisure to
   bother about whether you are happy or not. The
   cure for it is occupation.

George Bernard Shaw 1856–1950
Irish playwright

❦ Time is the great physician.

Benjamin Disraeli 1804–81
British Conservative politician and novelist

❦ Time has too much credit . . . It is not a great
healer. It is an indifferent and perfunctory
one. Sometimes it does not heal at all.
And sometimes when it seems to, no
healing has been necessary.

Ivy Compton-Burnett 1884–1969
English novelist

❦ We act as though comfort and luxury were the
chief requirements of life, when all we need to
make us really happy is something to be
enthusiastic about.

Charles Kingsley 1819–75
English writer and clergyman

❦ It is not true that suffering ennobles the
character; happiness does that sometimes,
but suffering, for the most part, makes men
petty and vindictive.

W. Somerset Maugham 1874–1965
English novelist

❦ Our sympathy is cold to the relation
of distant misery.

Edward Gibbon 1737–94
English historian

❦ I had become, with the approach of night,
once more aware of loneliness and time –
those two companions without whom no
journey can yield us anything.

Lawrence Durrell 1912–90
English writer

❧ Anything that consoles is fake.

Iris Murdoch 1919–99
English novelist

❧ Thirty years is a very long time to live
alone and life doesn't get any nicer.

Frances Partridge 1990—
English writer and diarist

❧ Depend upon it, if a man talks of his
misfortunes there is something in them that
is not disagreeable to him; for where there is
nothing but pure misery, there never is any
recourse to the mention of it.

Samuel Johnson 1709–84
English poet, critic and lexicographer

❧ He felt the loyalty we all feel to unhappiness –
the sense that that is where we really belong.

Graham Greene 1904–91
English novelist

❧ There is no more miserable human being
than one in whom nothing is habitual
but indecision.

William James 1842 1910
American philosopher

❧ Some men are born mediocre, some men
achieve mediocrity, and some men have
mediocrity thrust upon them. With
Major Major it had been all three.

Joseph Heller 1923–99
American novelist
(from *Catch-22*)

❧ There are minds so impatient of inferiority that
their gratitude is a species of revenge, and they
return benefits, not because recompense is a
pleasure, but because obligation is a pain.

Samuel Johnson 1709–84
English poet, critic and lexicographer

❧ If a madman were to come into this room with a
stick in his hand, no doubt we should pity the
state of his mind; but our primary consideration
would be to take care of ourselves. We should
knock him down first, and pity him afterwards.

Samuel Johnson 1709–84
English poet, critic and lexicographer

❧ How small and selfish is sorrow. But it
bangs one about until one is senseless.

Queen Elizabeth, the Queen Mother 1900–2002

❦ Sorrow is tranquillity remembered in emotion.

Dorothy Parker 1893–1967
American critic and humorist

❦ Keep violence in the mind, where is belongs.

Brian Aldiss 1925—
English science-fiction writer

❦ Nothing is more terrible than ignorance
with spurs on.

Johann Wolfgang von Goethe 1749–1832
German poet, novelist and playwright

❦ Bigotry may be roughly defined as the anger
of men who have no opinions.

G. K. Chesterton 1874–1936
English essayist, novelist and poet

❧ Like all weak men he laid an exaggerated stress on not changing one's mind.

W. Somerset Maugham 1874–1965
English novelist

❧ Mendacity is a system that we live in. Liquor is one way out an' death's the other.

Tennessee Williams 1911–83
American playwright

❧ A belief in a supernatural source of evil is not necessary; men alone are quite capable of every wickedness.

Joseph Conrad 1857–1924
Polish-born English novelist

❦ How to be one up [is] to make the other man
feel that something has gone wrong,
however slightly.

Stephen Potter 1900–69
British writer

❦ No one can make you feel inferior without
your consent.

Eleanor Roosevelt 1884–1962
American humanitarian and diplomat

❦ If only I could get down to Sidcup! I've been
waiting for the weather to break. He's got
my papers, this man I left them with,
it's got it all down there, I could
prove everything.

Harold Pinter 1930—
English playwright
(from *The Caretaker*)

❦ And suppose we solve all the problems it
  presents? What happens? We end up with
  more problems than we started with. Because
  that's the way problems propagate their species.
  A problem left to itself dries up or goes rotten.
  But fertilize a problem with a solution –
  you'll hatch out dozens.

N. F. Simpson 1919—
English playwright

❦ The growth of a large business is merely a
  survival of the fittest . . . The American Beauty
  rose can be produced in the splendour and
  fragrance which bring cheer to its beholder
  only by sacrificing the early buds which
  grow up around it.

John D. Rockefeller 1839–1937
American industrialist and philanthropist

❦ Someone has somewhere commented on the
fact that millions long for immortality who
don't know what to do with themselves on a
rainy Sunday afternoon.

Susan Ertz 1894–1985
American writer

· ❦ It was a Sunday afternoon, wet and cheerless:
and a duller spectacle this earth of ours has
not to show than a rainy Sunday in London.

Thomas De Quincey 1785–1859
English essayist and critic

❦ The feeling of Sunday is the same everywhere,
heavy, melancholy, standing still. Like when
they say, 'As it was in the beginning, is now,
and ever shall be, world without end.'

Jean Rhys c. 1890–1979
British novelist and short-story writer

❧ The black dog I hope always to resist . . .
though I am deprived of almost all those that
used to help me . . . When I rise my breakfast
is solitary, the black dog waits to share it; from
breakfast to dinner he continues barking,
except that Dr Brocklesby for a little keeps
him at a distance . . . Night comes at last,
and some hours of restlessness and confusion
bring me again to a day of solitude. What
shall exclude the black dog from a habitation
like this?

Samuel Johnson 1709–84
English poet, critic and lexicographer

❧ In a real dark night of the soul it is always three
o'clock in the morning.

F. Scott Fitzgerald 1896–1940
American novelist

❦ The chains of habit are too weak to be felt
   until they are too strong to be broken.

Samuel Johnson 1709–84
English poet, critic and lexicographer

❦ We love peace, as we abhor pusillanimity;
   but not peace at any price. There is a peace
   more destructive of the manhood of living
   man than war is destructive of his material
   body. Chains are worse than bayonets.

Douglas Jerrold 1803–57
English playwright and journalist

❦ You can't say civilization don't advance,
   however, for in every war they kill
   you in a new way.

Will Rogers 1879–1935
American actor and humorist

❦ Every position must be held to the last man:
   there must be no retirement. With our backs
   to the wall, and believing in the justice of our
   cause, each one of us must fight on to the end.

Earl Haig 1861–1928
(order to British troops, 12 April 1918)

❦ [Public schoolboys] go forth into a world that is
   not entirely composed of public-school men, or
   even of Anglo Saxons, but of men who are as
   various as the sands of the sea; into a world
   of whose richness and subtlety they have no
   conception. They go forth into it with well-
   developed bodies, fairly developed minds
   and undeveloped hearts.

E. M. Forster 1879–1970
English novelist

❧ If I have seen farther it is by standing on the shoulders of giants.

Sir Isaac Newton 1642–1727
English mathematician and physicist

❧ The reasonable man adapts himself to the world: the unreasonable one persists in trying to adapt the world to himself. Therefore all progress depends on the unreasonable man.

George Bernard Shaw 1856–1950
Irish playwright

❧ Poverty is no disgrace to a man, but it is confoundedly inconvenient.

Sydney Smith 1771–1845
English clergyman and essayist

❧ They had been corrupted by money, and he had been corrupted by sentiment. Sentiment was the more dangerous, because you couldn't name its price. A man open to bribes was to be relied upon below a certain figure, but sentiment might uncoil in the heart at a name, a photograph, even a smell remembered.

Graham Greene 1904–91
English novelist
(from *The Heart of the Matter*)

❧ Only in our virtues are we original, because virtue is difficult . . . Vices are general, virtues are particular.

Iris Murdoch 1919–99
English novelist

❧ Our names are labels plainly printed on the bottled essence of our past behaviour.

Logan Pearsall Smith 1865–1946
American-born British writer

❧ Each had his past shut in him like the leaves of a book known to him by heart; and his friends could only read the title.

Virginia Woolf 1882–1941
English novelist

❧ What is charm then? The free giving of a grace, the spending of something given by nature in her role as spendthrift . . . something extra, superfluous, unnecessary, essentially a power thrown away.

Doris Lessing 1919—
English writer

❦ Other people's lives may easily be human
documents. But a man's own life is
always a melodrama.

G. K. Chesterton 1874–1936
English essayist, novelist and poet

❦ People must not do things for fun. We are
not here for fun. There is no reference to
fun in any Act of Parliament.

A. P. Herbert 1890–1971
English writer and humorist

❦ Has it ever struck you that there's a thin man
inside every fat man, just as they say there's
a statue inside every block of stone?

George Orwell 1903–50
English novelist

❦ In every age of transition men are never so
firmly bound to one way of life as when they
are about to abandon it, so that fanaticism and
intolerance reach their most intense forms
just before tolerance and mutual acceptance
come to be the natural order of things.

Bernard Levin 1928—
British journalist

❦ We live in a fantasy world, a world of illusion.
The great task in life is to find reality.

Iris Murdoch 1919–99
English novelist

❦ Security is when everything is settled, when
nothing can happen to you; security is the
denial of life.

Germaine Greer 1939—
Australian feminist

❧ If once a man indulges himself in murder, very soon he comes to think little of robbing; and from robbing he comes next to drinking and Sabbath-breaking, and from that to incivility and procrastination.

Thomas De Quincey 1785–1859
English essayist and critic

❧ Is it possible to succeed without any act of betrayal?

Jean Renoir 1894–1979
French film director

❧ History . . . is, indeed, little more than the register of the crimes, follies and misfortunes of mankind.

Edward Gibbon 1737–94
English historian

❧ Any victim demands allegiance.

Graham Greene 1904–91
English novelist

❧ Hypocrisy is the most difficult and nerve-racking vice that any man can pursue; it needs an unceasing vigilance and a rare detachment of spirit. It cannot, like adultery or gluttony, be practised at spare moments; it is a whole-time job.

W. Somerset Maugham 1874–1965
English novelist

❧ Far from being the basis of the good society, the family, with its narrow privacy and tawdry secrets, is the source of all our discontents.

Edmund Leach 1910—
English anthropologist

The moral flabbiness born of the exclusive worship of the bitch-goddess success. That – with the squalid cash interpretation put on the word success – is our national disease.

William James 1842–1910
American philosopher

The Balloon of
Experience

❦ The balloon of experience is in fact of course
tied to the earth, and under that necessity we
swing, thanks to a rope of remarkable length,
in the more or less commodious car of the
imagination; but it is by the rope we know
where we are, and from the moment that
cable is cut we are at large and unrelated.

Henry James 1843–1916
American novelist

❦ Swimming for his life, a man does not
see much of the country through which
the river winds.

W. E. Gladstone 1809–98
British Liberal politician

❧ It is queer how it is always one's virtues
and not one's vices that precipitate one
into disaster.

Rebecca West 1892–1983
English novelist and journalist

❧ The world is divided into people who do
things and people who get the credit.
Try, if you can, to belong to the first
class. There's far less competition.

Dwight Morrow 1873–1931
American lawyer, banker and diplomat

❧ Death and taxes and childbirth! There's
never a convenient time for any of them.

Margaret Mitchell 1900–49
American novelist

❧ The awe and dread with which the untutored
savage contemplates his mother-in-law are
amongst the most familiar facts of
anthropology.

James George Frazer 1854–1941
Scottish anthropologist

❧ Down these mean streets a man must go
who is not himself mean, who is neither
tarnished nor afraid.

Raymond Chandler 1888–1959
American writer of detective fiction

❧ Life is a foreign language: all men
mispronounce it.

Christopher Morley 1890–1957
American writer

❧ Every generation revolts against its fathers and makes friends with its grandfathers.

Lewis Mumford 1895–1990
American sociologist

❧ Any man who hates dogs and babies can't be all bad.

Leo Rosten 1908—
American writer and social scientist
(of W. C. Fields, and often attributed to him)

❧ A loud noise at one end and no sense of responsibility at the other.

Ronald Knox 1888–1957
English writer and Roman Catholic priest
(definition of a baby)

❧ Love set you going like a fat gold watch.
   The midwife slapped your footsoles, and your
                                        bald cry
   Took its place among the elements.

Sylvia Plath 1932–63
American poet

❧ There is no finer investment for any
   community than putting milk into babies.

Winston Churchill 1874–1965
British Conservative politician

❧ Every luxury was lavished on you – atheism,
   breast-feeding, circumcision.

Joe Orton 1933–67
English playwright
(from *Loot*)

❧ In America there are two classes of travel –
first class and with children.

Robert Benchley 1889–1945
American humorist

❧ The thing that impresses me most about
America is the way parents obey their children.

Edward VIII (Duke of Windsor) 1894–1972

❧ Sow an act, and you reap a habit. Sow a habit,
and you reap a character. Sow a character,
and you reap a destiny.

Charles Reade 1814–84
English novelist and playwright

❦ From the earliest times, the old have rubbed it
   into the young that they are wiser than they,
   and before the young had discovered what
   nonsense this was they were old too, and it
   profited them to carry on the imposture.

W. Somerset Maugham 1874–1965
English novelist

❦ Years ago, manhood was an opportunity
   for achievement, and now it is a problem
   to be overcome.

Garrison Keillor 1942—
American humorous writer

❦ Better build schoolrooms for the boy,
   than cells and gibbets for the man.

Eliza Cook 1818–89
English poet

❧ Good gracious, you've got to educate him first.
You can't expect a boy to be vicious till he's
been to a good school.

Saki (Hector Hugh Munro) 1870–1916
Scottish writer

❧ Teach him to think for himself? Oh, my God,
teach him rather to think like other people!

Mary Shelley 1797 1851
English novelist

❧ Few misfortunes can befall a boy which bring
worse consequences than to have a really
affectionate mother.

W. Somerset Maugham 1874–1965
English novelist

❦ A nickname is the heaviest stone that
the devil can throw at a man.

William Hazlitt 1778–1830
English essayist

❦ The name of a man is a numbing blow
from which he never recovers.

Marshall McLuhan 1911–80
Canadian communications scholar

❦ There is always one moment in childhood
when the door opens and lets the
future in.

Graham Greene 1904–91
English novelist

❧ At school I never minded the lessons.
I just resented having to work terribly
hard at playing.

John Mortimer 1923—
English novelist, barrister and playwright

❧ Oh my! Bertha's got a bang on the boko. Keep
a stiff upper lip, Bertha dear. What, knocked
a tooth out? Never mind, dear, laugh it off,
laugh it off; it's all part of life's rich pageant.

Arthur Marshall 1910–89
British journalist and former schoolmaster
(from *The Games Mistress*)

❧ I'd the upbringing a nun would envy . . .
Until I was fifteen I was more familiar
with Africa than my own body.

Joe Orton 1933–67
English playwright

❦ Being an old maid is like death by drowning,
   a really delightful sensation after you cease
   to struggle.

Edna Ferber 1887–1968
American writer

❦ Somehow a bachelor never quite gets over
   the idea that he is a thing of beauty and
   a boy forever.

Helen Rowland 1875–1950
American writer

❦ You can't learn too soon that the most useful
   thing about a principle is that it can always
   be sacrificed to expediency.

W. Somerset Maugham 1874–1965
English novelist

❧ Success reveals infirmities which failure
   would otherwise conceal.

John Stuart Mill 1806–73
English philosopher and social reformer

❧ A pessimist is a man who has been compelled
   to live with an optimist.

Elbert Hubbard 1859–1915
American writer

❧ The optimist proclaims that we live in the best
   of all possible worlds; and the pessimist fears
   that this is true.

James Branch Cabell 1879–1958
American novelist and essayist

❦ For of all sad words of tongue or pen,
  The saddest are these: 'It might have been!'

John Greeleaf Whittier 1807–92
American poet

❦ No man is rich enough to buy back his past.

Oscar Wilde 1854–1900
Anglo-Irish playwright and poet

❦ I learned . . . that one can never go back, that
  one should not ever try to go back – that the
  essence of life is going forward. Life is really a
  one-way street.

Agatha Christie 1890–1976
English writer of detective fiction

❦ I expect to pass through this world but once;
any good thing therefore that I can do, or any
kindness that I can show to any fellow-creature,
let me do it now; let me not defer or neglect it,
for I shall not pass this way again.

Stephen Grellet 1773–1855
French missionary

❦ It's only those who do nothing that make no
mistakes, I suppose.

Joseph Conrad 1857–1924
Polish-born English novelist

❦ Don't talk to me about naval tradition. It's
nothing but rum, sodomy and the lash.

Winston Churchill 1874–1965
British Conservative politician

❧ Many a man has a bonfire in his heart and nobody comes to warm himself at it. The passers-by notice only a little smoke coming from the chimney and go away.

Vincent Van Gogh 1853–90
Dutch painter

❧ As a general rule, philosophy is like stirring mud or not letting sleeping dogs lie.

Samuel Butler 1835–1902
English novelist

❧ There was no need to do any housework at all. After the first four years the dirt doesn't get any worse.

Quentin Crisp 1908–99
English writer

❦   A man who could make so vile a pun would
    not scruple to pick a pocket.

John Dennis 1657–1734
English critic, poet and playwright

❦   There are three kinds of lies: lies, damned lies
    and statistics.

Benjamin Disraeli 1804–81
British Conservative politician and novelist

❦   To trust people is a luxury in which only the
    wealthy can indulge; the poor cannot afford it.

E. M. Forster 1879–1970
English novelist

❦   And always keep a-hold of Nurse
    For fear of finding something worse.

Hilaire Belloc 1870–1953
French-born British writer and poet

❧ Innocence always calls mutely for protection, when we would be so much wiser to guard ourselves against it: innocence is like a dumb leper who has lost his bell, wandering the world meaning no harm.

Graham Greene 1904–91
English novelist

❧ Never stop because you are afraid – you are never so likely to be wrong. Never keep a line of retreat: it is a wretched invention. The difficult is what takes a little time; the impossible is what takes a little longer.

Fridtjof Nansen 1861–1930
Norwegian polar explorer

❧ Misers are very kind people: they amass
wealth for those who wish their death.

Stanislaus, King of Poland 1677–1766

❧ Money is better than poverty, if only for
financial reasons.

Woody Allen 1935—
American film director, writer and actor

❧ People don't resent having nothing nearly
as much as too little.

Ivy Compton-Burnett 1884–1969
English novelist

❧ Expenditure rises to meet income.

C. Northcote Parkinson 1909–93
English writer

❦ A broker is a man who takes your fortune
and runs it into a shoestring.

Alexander Woollcott 1887–1943
American writer

❦ Economy is going without something you do
want in case you should some day want
something you probably won't want.

Anthony Hope 1863–1933
English novelist

❦ Half our life is spent trying to find something
to do with the time we have rushed through
life trying to save.

Will Rogers 1879–1935
American actor and humorist

❧ Moral indignation is jealousy with a halo.

H. G. Wells 1866–1946
English novelist

❧ Shallow brooks murmur most,
deep silent slide away.

Sir Philip Sidney 1554–86
English soldier, poet and courtier

❧ Better a live sparrow than a stuffed eagle.

Edward FitzGerald 1809–83
English scholar and poet

❧ Madness need not be all breakdown. It may also
be breakthrough.

R. D. Laing 1927–89
Scottish psychiatrist

❧ Fleas know not whether they are upon the body
  of a giant or upon one of ordinary size.

> Walter Savage Landor 1775–1864
> English poet

❧ To the Puritan all things are impure, as
  somebody says.

> D. H. Lawrence 1885–1930
> English novelist and poet

❧ Life is like a sewer. What you get out of it
  depends on what you put into it.

> Tom Lehrer 1928—
> American humorist

❧ The trumpets came out brazenly with the last
post. We all swallowed our spittle, chokingly,
while our eyes smarted against our wills. A
man hates to be moved to folly by a noise.

T. E. Lawrence 1888–1935
English soldier and writer

❧ I might give my life for my friend, but he had
better not ask me to do up a parcel.

Logan Pearsall Smith 1865–1946
American-born man of letters

❧ Cheer up! The worst is yet to come!

Philander Chase Johnson 1866–1939

❦ I do not believe that friends are necessarily
the people you like best, they are merely
the people who got there first.

Peter Ustinov 1921—
Russian-born actor, director and writer

❦ A self-made man is one who believes in luck
and sends his son to Oxford.

Christina Stead 1902–83
Australian novelist

❦ Good news seldom arrives in a buff envelope.

Anonymous

❦ Hope is a good breakfast, but it is a bad supper.

Francis Bacon 1561–1626
English philosopher and essayist

❦ Only the hopeless are starkly sincere and . . .
only the unhappy can either give or
take sympathy.

Jean Rhys c. 1890–1979
British novelist and short-story writer

❦ Morris read through the letter. Was it a shade
too fulsome? No, that was another law of
academic life: it is impossible to be excessive
in flattery of one's peers.

David Lodge 1935—
English novelist
(from Small World)

❦ I believe in getting into hot water – it helps
keep you clean.

G. K. Chesterton 1874–1936
English essayist, novelist and poet

❧ The roulette table pays nobody except him that keeps it. Nevertheless, a passion for gambling is common, though a passion for keeping roulette tables is unknown.

George Bernard Shaw 1856–1950
Irish playwright

❧ The follies which a man regrets most, in his life, are those which he didn't commit when he had the opportunity.

Helen Rowland 1875–1950
American writer

❧ The man who is denied the opportunity of taking decisions of importance begins to regard as important the decisions he is allowed to take.

C. Northcote Parkinson 1909–93
English writer

❦ It is rarely possible to carry the torch of truth through a crowd without singeing somebody's beard.

Joshua Bruyn

❦ The dust of exploded beliefs may make a fine sunset.

Geoffrey Madan 1895–1947
English bibliophile

❦ More people are flattered into virtue than bullied out of vice.

R. S. Surtees 1805–64
English sporting journalist and novelist

❧ Major Strasser has been shot. Round up
the usual suspects.

Julius J. Epstein 1909—
(from the film *Casablanca*)

❧ In a hierarchy every employee tends to rise
to his level of incompetence.

Laurence Peter 1919—
Canadian writer

❧ Never blow your own trumpet: if you do that,
other people will be loth to do it for you.

Max Beerbohm 1872–1956
English critic, essayist and caricaturist

❦ It is a good rule in life never to apologise.
The right sort of people do not want
apologies, and the wrong sort take a
mean advantage of them.

P. G. Wodehouse 1881–1975
English writer

❦ The world is becoming like a lunatic
asylum run by lunatics.

David Lloyd George 1863–1945
British Liberal politician

❦ Advertising is the rattling of a stick
inside a swill bucket.

George Orwell 1903–50
English novelist

❦ To say that these men paid their shillings to
watch twenty-two hirelings kick a ball is merely
to say that a violin is wood and catgut, that
Hamlet is so much paper and ink. For a
shilling the Bruddersford United AFC
offered you Conflict and Art.

J. B. Priestley 1894–1984
English novelist, playwright and critic

❦ Some people think football is a matter of
life and death . . . I can assure them it
is much more serious than that.

Bill Shankly 1914–81
Scottish footballer

❦ A sportsman is a man who, every now and then, simply has to get out and kill something. Not that he's cruel. He wouldn't hurt a fly. It's not big enough.

Stephen Leacock 1869–1944
Canadian humorist

❦ Serious sport has nothing to do with fair play. It is bound up with hatred, jealousy, boastfulness and disregard of all the rules.

George Orwell 1903–50
English novelist

❦ Some people get lost in thought because it is unfamiliar territory.

Anonymous

❧ The point is that nobody likes having salt
rubbed into their wounds, even if it is
the salt of the earth.

Rebecca West 1892–1983
English novelist and journalist

❧ The spirit of self-help is the root of all genuine
growth in the individual.

Samuel Smiles 1812–1904
English writer

❧ When people will not weed their own minds,
they are apt to be overrun with nettles.

Horace Walpole 1717–97
English writer and connoisseur

❦ Who shoots at the midday sun, though he be
sure, he shall never hit the mark; yet, as sure
he is, he shall shoot higher than he who
aims but at a bush.

Sir Philip Sidney 1554–86
English soldier, poet and courtier

❦ A little inaccuracy sometimes saves tons
of explanation.

Saki (Hector Hugh Munro) 1870–1916
Scottish writer

❦ In examinations those who do not wish
to know ask questions of those who
cannot tell.

Sir Walter Raleigh 1861–1922
English lecturer and critic

❧ In the culture I grew up in you did your work and did not put your arm around it to stop other people from looking. You took the earliest possible opportunity to make knowledge available.

James Black 1924—
British analytical pharmacologist

❧ In skating over thin ice, our safety is in our speed.

Ralph Waldo Emerson 1803–82
American philosopher and poet

❧ Education is what survives when what has been learned has been forgotten.

B. F. Skinner 1904–90
American psychologist

❦ Work expands so as to fill the time
   available for its completion.

C. Northcote Parkinson 1909–93
English writer

❦ Man is the only creature that consumes
   without producing.

George Orwell 1903–50
English novelist

❦ War hath no fury like a non-combatant.

C. E. Montague 1867–1928
British writer

❦ The car has become an article of dress
without which we feel uncertain, unclad
and incomplete in the urban compound.

Marshall McLuhan 1911–80
Canadian communications scholar

❦ No man, not even a doctor, ever gives any
other definition of what a nurse should be
than this – 'devoted and obedient'. This
definition would do just as well for a porter.
It might even do for a horse. It would not
do for a policeman.

Florence Nightingale 1820–1910
English nurse

❦ Policemen, like red squirrels, must
be protected.

Joe Orton 1933–67
English playwright

❦ Be nice to people on your way up because
you'll meet 'em on your way down.

Wilson Mizner 1876–1933
American playwright

❦ People ask you for criticism, but they only
want praise.

W. Somerset Maugham 1874–1965
English novelist

❦ Imprisoned in every fat man a thin one
is wildly signalling to be let out.

Cyril Connolly 1903–74
English writer

❦ Life, if you're fat, is a minefield – you have to
pick your way, otherwise you blow up.

Miriam Margolyes 1940—
English actress

❧ Nothing, like something, happens anywhere.

Philip Larkin 1922–85
English poet

❧ Some people are so fond of ill-luck that
they run halfway to meet it.

Douglas Jerrold 1803–57
English playwright and journalist

❧ The art of being wise is the art of knowing
what to overlook.

William James 1842–1910
American philosopher

❧ A bank is a place that will lend you money
if you can prove that you don't need it.

Bob Hope 1903—
American comedian

❦ Grace under pressure.

Ernest Hemingway 1899–1961
American novelist
(when asked what he meant by 'guts')

❦ There is an unseemly exposure of the
mind, as well as of the body.

William Hazlitt 1778–1830
English essayist

❦ A verbal contract isn't worth the paper
it is written on.

Sam Goldwyn 1882–1974
American film producer

❦ Genius is one per cent inspiration, ninety-nine
per cent perspiration.

Thomas Alva Edison 1847–1931
American inventor

❦ We feel free when we escape – even if it be but from the frying pan into the fire.

Eric Hoffer 1902–83
American philosopher

❦ Freud's theory was that when a joke opens a window and all those bats and bogeymen fly out, you get a marvellous feeling of relief and elation. The trouble with Freud is that he never had to play the old Glasgow Empire on a Saturday night after Rangers and Celtic had both lost.

Ken Dodd 1931—
British comedian

Life, the Universe and Everything

❧ The answer to the great question of . . . life, the universe and everything . . . [is] forty-two.

Douglas Adams 1952–2001
(*The Hitchhiker's Guide to the Galaxy*)

❧ The essence of life is statistical improbability on a colossal scale.

Richard Dawkins 1941—
English biologist

❧ I don't know what I may seem to the world, but as to myself, I seem to have been only like a boy playing on the seashore and diverting myself in now and then finding a smoother pebble or a prettier shell than ordinary, whilst the great ocean of truth lay all undiscovered before me.

Isaac Newton 1642–1727
English mathematician and physicist

❦ There are one hundred and ninety-three living
species of monkeys and apes. One hundred
and ninety-two of them are covered with
hair. The exception is a naked ape
self-named *Homo sapiens*.

Desmond Morris 1928—
English anthropologist

❦ Man, biologically considered, and whatever else
he may be into the bargain, is simply the most
formidable of all the beasts of prey, and, indeed,
the only one that preys systematically on its
own species.

William James 1842–1910
American philosopher

❦ Well, of course, people are only human . . . But
it really does not seem much for them to be.

Ivy Compton-Burnett 1884–1969
English novelist

❦ A man that is born falls into a dream like a
man who falls into the sea. If he tries to
climb out into the air as inexperienced
people endeavour to do, he drowns . . . to
the destructive element submit yourself,
and with the exertions of your hands
and feet in the water make the deep,
deep sea keep you up.

Joseph Conrad 1857–1924
Polish-born English novelist

❦ I am standing on the threshold about to enter a room. It is a complicated business. In the first place I must shove against an atmosphere pressing with a force of fourteen pounds on every square inch of my body. I must make sure of landing on a plank travelling at twenty miles a second round the sun – a fraction of a second too early or too late, the plank would be miles away. I must do this whilst hanging from a round planet, head outward into space, and with a wind of aether blowing at no one knows how many miles a second through every interstice of my body.

Arthur Eddington 1882–1944
British astrophysicist

❦ They are in you and in me, they created us, body and mind; and their preservation is the ultimate rationale for our existence . . . they go by the name of genes, and we are their survival machines.

Richard Dawkins 1941—
English biologist

❦ Life is a maze in which we take the wrong turning before we have learnt to walk.

Cyril Connolly 1903–74
English writer

❦ However many ways there may be of being alive, it is certain that there are vastly more ways of being dead.

Richard Dawkins 1941—
English biologist

❦ I saw the best minds of my generation
destroyed by madness, starving, hysterical,
naked, dragging themselves through the
Negro streets at dawn looking for an angry
fix, angel-headed hipsters burning for the
ancient heavenly connection to the starry
dynamo in the machinery of the night.

Allen Ginsberg 1926–97
American poet and novelist

❦ In effect, we have redefined the task of science
to be the discovery of laws that will enable
us to predict events up to the limits set
by the uncertainty principle.

Stephen Hawking 1942—
English theoretical physicist

❦ In the nineteenth century the problem was
that God is dead; in the twentieth century the
problem is that man is dead. In the nineteenth
century inhumanity meant cruelty; in the
twentieth century is means schizoid self-
alienation. The danger of the past was
that men became slaves. The danger of
the future is that men may become robots.

Erich Fromm 1900–80
American philosopher and psychologist

❦ If a little knowledge is dangerous, where is
the man who has so much as to be out
of danger?

T. H. Huxley 1825–95
English biologist

❧ I have tried at various times in my life to grasp the rudiments of such inventions as the telephone, the camera, wireless telegraphy and even the ordinary motor car, but without success.

Television, of course, and radar and atomic energy are so far beyond my comprehension that my brain shudders at the thought of them and scurries for cover like a primitive tribesman confronted for the first time with a Dunhill cigarette lighter.

Noël Coward 1899–1973
English playwright, actor and composer

❧ Is it progress if a cannibal uses knife and fork?

Stanislaw Lec 1909–66
Polish writer

If my theory of relativity is proven correct,
Germany will claim me as a German and
France will declare that I am a citizen of
the world. Should my theory prove untrue,
France will say that I am a German and
Germany will declare that I am a Jew.

Albert Einstein 1879–1955
German-born theoretical physicist

Apart from the known and the unknown, what
else is there?

Harold Pinter 1930—
English playwright

I didn't go to the moon, I went much farther –
for time is the longest distance between
two places.

Tennessee Williams 1911–83
American playwright

❧ Shakespeare would have grasped wave functions, Donne would have understood complementarity and relative time. They would have been excited. What richness! They would have plundered this new science for their imagery. And they would have educated their audiences too. But you 'arts' people, you're not only ignorant of these magnificent things, you're rather proud of knowing nothing.

Ian McEwan 1948—
English novelist

❧ The new electronic interdependence recreates the world in the image of a global village.

Marshall McLuhan 1911–80
Canadian communications scholar

❦ Let us record the atoms as they fall upon the mind in the order in which they fall, let us trace the pattern, however disconnected and incoherent in appearance, which each sight or incident scores upon the consciousness. Let us not take it for granted that life exists more fully in what is commonly thought big than in what is commonly thought small.

Virginia Woolf 1882–1941
English novelist

❦ What peaches and what penumbras! Whole families shopping at night! Aisles full of husbands! Wives in the avocados, babies in the tomatoes! – and you, Garcia Lorca, what were you doing down by the watermelons?

Allen Ginsberg 1926–97
American poet and novelist

❧ I keep picturing all these little kids playing some game in this big field of rye and all . . . I mean if they're running and they don't look where they're going I have to come out from somewhere and catch them. That's all I'd do all day. I'd just be the catcher in the rye.

J. D. Salinger 1919–
American novelist and short-story writer
(from *The Catcher in the Rye*)

❧ If you want truth to go round the world you must hire an express train to pull it; but if you want a lie to go round the world, it will fly: it is as light as a feather, and a breath will carry it. It is well said in the old proverb, 'A lie will go round the world while truth is pulling its boots on.'

C. H. Spurgeon 1834–92
English nonconformist preacher

❦ Time spent on any item of the agenda will be in inverse proportion to the sum involved.

C. Northcote Parkinson 1909–93
English writer

❦ I feel like a fugitive from th' law of averages.

Bill Mauldin 1921–2003
American cartoonist

❦ We started off trying to set up a small anarchist community, but people wouldn't obey the rules.

Alan Bennett 1934—
English actor and playwright

❦ Gentlemen, include me out.

Sam Goldwyn 1882–1974
American film producer

❦ The Common Law of England has been
laboriously built about a mythical figure –
the figure of 'The Reasonable Man'.

A. P. Herbert 1890–1971
English writer and humorist

❦ Examine for a moment an ordinary mind
on an ordinary day.

Virginia Woolf 1882–1941
English novelist

❦ What if someone gave a war & nobody came?
Life would ring the bells of ecstasy and for ever
be itself again.

Allen Ginsberg 1926–97
American poet and novelist

❦ What is official is incontestable. It undercuts
the problematical world and sells us life at a
discount.

Christopher Fry 1907—
English playwright

❦ There was a pause – just long enough for an
angel to pass, flying slowly.

Ronald Firbank 1886–1926
English novelist

❦ Small earthquake in Chile. Not many dead.

Claud Cockburn 1904–81
British writer and journalist
(the words which won a competition at
The Times for the dullest headline)

❧ You have not had thirty years' experience . . .
You have had one year's experience
thirty times.

J. L. Carr 1912–94
English novelist

❧ I am a sundial, and I make a botch
Of what is done much better by a watch.

Hilaire Belloc 1870–1953
French-born British writer and poet

❧ Only connect! . . . Only connect the prose
and the passion, and both will be exalted,
and human love will be seen at its height.

E. M. Forster 1879–1970
English novelist

❦ Detection is, or ought to be, an exact science, and should be treated in the same cold and unemotional manner. You have attempted to tinge it with romanticism, which produces much the same effect as if you worked a love-story or an elopement into the fifth proposition of Euclid.

Sir Arthur Conan Doyle 1859–1930
Scottish-born writer

❦ The interpretation of dreams is the royal road to a knowledge of the unconscious activities of the mind.

Sigmund Freud 1856–1939
Austrian psychiatrist

❦ Minds are like parachutes, they only
   function when they are open.

James Dewar 1842–1923
Scottish physicist

❦ Our memories are card-indexes consulted,
   and then put back in disorder by authorities
   whom we do not control.

Cyril Connolly 1903–74
English writer

❦ Many a genius has been slow of growth. Oaks
   that flourish for a thousand years do not spring
   up into beauty like a reed.

G. H. Lewes 1817–78
English man of letters

❦ If A is a success in life, then A equals x plus y plus z. Work is x; y is play; and z is keeping your mouth shut.

Albert Einstein 1879–1955
German-born theoretical physicist

❦ A man should keep his little brain attic stocked with all the furniture that he is likely to use, and the rest he can put away in the lumber room of his library, where he can get it if he wants it.

Sir Arthur Conan Doyle 1859–1930
Scottish-born writer

❦ Rowe's Rule: the odds are five to six that the light at the end of the tunnel is the headlight of an oncoming train.

Paul Dickson 1939—
American writer

🍃 There was only one catch and that was Catch-22, which specified that a concern for one's own safety in the face of dangers that were real and immediate was the process of a rational mind . . . Orr would be crazy to fly more missions and sane if he didn't, but if he was sane he had to fly them. If he flew them he was crazy and didn't have to; but if he didn't want to he was sane and had to.

Joseph Heller 1923–99
American novelist
(from *Catch-22*)

🍃 Human beings have an inalienable right to invent themselves; when that right is pre-empted it is called brainwashing.

Germaine Greer 1939—
Australian feminist

❧ [I wanted] to discover what lies behind the
dark, thick leaf of the aspidistra that guards . . .
the vulnerable gap between the lace curtains.

Graham Greene 1904–91
English novelist

❧ [There are] only two classes of pedestrians
in these days of reckless motor traffic –
the quick and the dead.

Lord Dewar 1864–1930
British industrialist

❧ Dr Strabismus (whom God preserve) of Utrecht
has patented a new invention. It is an
illuminated trouser-clip for bicyclists who are
using main roads at night.

J. B. Morton ('Beachcomber') 1893–1975
British journalist

❦ Lord Finchley tried to mend the electric light
Himself. It struck him dead: and serve

him right!

It is the business of the wealthy man
To give employment to the artisan.

Hilaire Belloc 1870–1953
French-born British writer and poet

❦ My only solution for the problem of habitual
accidents . . . is to stay in bed all day. Even
then, there is always the chance that you
will fall out.

Robert Benchley 1889–1945
American humorist

❦ Where in this small-talking world can I find a
longitude with no platitude?

Christopher Fry 1907—
English playwright

❧ No man will be a sailor who has contrivance
enough to get himself into a gaol; for being
in a ship is being in a gaol, with the chance
of being drowned . . . A man in a gaol has
more room, better food, and commonly
better company.

Samuel Johnson 1709–84
English poet, critic and lexicographer

A Trout in
the Milk

❧ Some circumstantial evidence is very strong, as when you find a trout in the milk.

Henry David Thoreau 1817-62
American writer

❧ Once the toothpaste is out of the tube, it is awfully hard to get it back in.

H. R. Haldeman 1929—
Presidential assistant to Richard Nixon

❧ I had never had a piece of toast
Particularly long and wide,
But fell upon the sanded floor,
And always on the buttered side.

James Payn 1830–98
English writer

❦ 'No hurry, no hurry,' said Sir James, with that air of self-denial that conveys the urgent necessity of intense speed.

Ada Leverson 1865–1936
English novelist

❦ It is better to entertain an idea than to take it home to live with you for the rest of your life.

William James 1842–1910
American philosopher

❦ There's sand in the porridge and sand in
                              the bed,
And if this is pleasure we'd rather be dead.

Noël Coward 1899–1973
English playwright, actor and composer

❦ Come forth, Lazarus! And he came fifth and lost the job.

James Joyce 1882–1941
Irish novelist

❦ I called off his players' names as they came marching up the steps behind him . . . All nice guys. They'll finish last. Nice guys finish last.

Leo Durocher 1906–91
American baseball coach

❦ In the midst of life we are in debt.

Ethel Watts Mumford 1878–1940

❧ Life is something to do when you can't
get to sleep.

Fran Lebowitz 1946—
American writer

❧ I would live all my life in nonchalance and
insouciance
Were it not for making a living, which is
rather a nouciance.

Ogden Nash 1902–71
American humorist

❧ It is impossible to enjoy idling thoroughly
unless one has plenty of work to do.

Jerome K. Jerome 1859–1927
English writer

❧ A perpetual holiday is a good working
definition of hell.

George Bernard Shaw 1856–1950
Irish playwright

❧ The landlady of a boarding-house is a
parallelogram – that is, an oblong figure,
which cannot be described, but which
is equal to anything.

Stephen Leacock 1869–1944
Canadian humorist

❧ Of all noxious animals . . . the most noxious
is a tourist. And of all tourists the most
vulgar, ill-bred, offensive and loathsome
is the British tourist.

Francis Kilvert 1840–79
English clergyman and diarist

❧ I want a house that has got over all its
troubles; I don't want to spend the rest
of my life bringing up a young and
inexperienced house.

Jerome K. Jerome 1859–1927
English writer

❧ 'There's been an accident,' they said,
'Your servant's cut in half; he's dead!'
'Indeed!' said Mr Jones, 'and please,
Send me the half that's got my keys.'

Harry Graham 1874–1936
British writer and journalist

❦ The march of mind has marched in through my back parlour shutters, and out again with my silver spoons, in the dead of night. The policeman, who was sent down to examine, says my house has been broken open on the most scientific principles.

Thomas Love Peacock 1785–1866
English novelist and poet

❦ JUDGE: What do you suppose I am on the Bench for, Mr Smith?

SMITH: It is not for me, Your Honour, to attempt to fathom the inscrutable workings of Providence.

F. E. Smith 1872–1930
British Conservative politician and lawyer

🐦 The law seems like a sort of maze through
which a client must be led to safety, a
collection of reefs, rocks and underwater
hazards through which he or she must
be piloted.

John Mortimer 1923—
English novelist, barrister and playwright

🐦 There are no handles to a horse, but the 1910
model has a string to each side of its face for
turning its head when there is anything
you want it to see.

Stephen Leacock 1869–1944
Canadian humorist

🐦 Milk's leap toward immortality.

Clifton Fadiman 1904–99
American writer
(of cheese)

❧ The pellet with the poison's in the vessel with the pestle. The chalice from the palace has the brew that is true.

Norman Panama 1914— and Melvin Frank 1913–88
American screenwriters
(from the film *The Court Jester*)

❧ Why is it no one ever sent me yet
One perfect limousine, do you suppose?
Ah no, it's always just my luck to get
One perfect rose.

Dorothy Parker 1893–1967
American critic and humorist

❧ Billy, in one of his nice new sashes,
  Fell in the fire and was burnt to ashes;
  Now, although the room grows chilly,
  I haven't the heart to poke poor Billy.

Harry Graham 1874–1936
British writer and journalist

❧ 'Whom are you?' he asked, for he had attended
  business college.

George Ade 1866–1944
American humorist and playwright

❧ JUDGE: You are extremely offensive, young man.
  SMITH: As a matter of fact, we both are, and
  the only difference between us is that I am
  trying to be, and you can't help it.

F. E. Smith 1872–1930
British Conservative politician and lawyer

❧ You will put on a dress of guilt and shoes with broken high ideals.

Roger McGough 1937—
English poet

❧ A healthy male adult bore consumes each year one and a half times his own weight in other people's patience.

John Updike 1932—
American novelist and short-story writer

❧ What is the victory of a cat on a hot tin roof? – I wish I knew . . . just staying on it, I guess, as long as she can.

Tennessee Williams 1911–83
American playwright

❦ Weep not for little Léonie
   Abducted by a French marquis!
   Though loss of honour was a wrench
   Just think how it's improved her French.

Harry Graham 1874–1936
British writer and journalist

❦ I used to be Snow White . . . but I drifted.

Mae West 1892–1980
American film actress

❦ [Irritable judges] suffer from a bad case of
   premature adjudication.

John Mortimer 1923—
English novelist, barrister and playwright

❧ Any man who goes to a psychiatrist should have his head examined.

Sam Goldwyn 1882–1974
American film producer

❧ Money is like a sixth sense without which you cannot make a complete use of the other five.

W. Somerset Maugham 1874–1965
English novelist

❧ My poor fellow, why not carry a watch?

Herbert Beerbohm Tree 1852–1917
English actor-manager
(to a man in the street, carrying a grandfather clock)

❧ We even sell a pair of earrings for under a
   pound, which is cheaper than a prawn
   sandwich from Marks & Spencers. But
   I have to say the earrings probably
   won't last as long.

Gerald Ratner 1949—
English businessman

❧ Ice formed on the butler's upper slopes.

P. G. Wodehouse 1881–1975
English writer

❧ Simple people suffer from mothers-in-law;
   intellectuals from daughters-in-law.

Anton Chekhov 1860–1904
Russian playwright and short-story writer

❧ Against the beautiful and the clever and the successful, one can wage a pitiless war, but not against the unattractive.

Graham Greene 1904–91
English novelist

❧ Wit is like caviare. It should be served in small, elegant portions and not splashed about like marmalade.

Noël Coward 1899–1973
English playwright, actor and composer

❧ No brilliance is needed in the law. Nothing but common sense, and relatively clean fingernails.

John Mortimer 1923—
English novelist, barrister and playwright

❦ When seagulls follow a trawler, it is because they think sardines will be thrown into the sea.

Eric Cantona 1966—
French footballer

❦ 'About the termination of pregnancy – I want your opinion. The father was syphilitic. The mother tuberculous. Of the children born, the first was blind, the second died, the third was deaf and dumb, the fourth was tuberculous. What would you have done?'

'I would have ended the next pregnancy.'

'Then you would have murdered Beethoven.'

Maurice Baring 1874–1945
English man of letters

Fly fishing may be a very pleasant amusement; but angling or float fishing I can only compare to a stick and a string with a worm at one end and a fool at the other.

Samuel Johnson 1709–84
English poet, critic and lexicographer

Under the
Moorish Wall

❦ He kissed me under the Moorish wall and I
thought well as well him as another and then I
asked him with my eyes to ask again yes and
then he asked me would I yes to say yes my
mountain flower and first I put my arms
around him yes and drew him down to me so
he could feel my breasts all perfume yes and
his heart was going like mad and yes I said yes
I will Yes.

James Joyce 1882–1941
Irish novelist
(from *Ulysses*)

❦ Wooing, so tiring.

Nancy Mitford 1904–73
English writer

❦ There is a middle state between love and
friendship more delightful than either but
more difficult to remain in.

Walter Savage Landor 1775–1864
English poet

❦ Man's love is of man's life a thing apart,
'Tis woman's whole existence.

Lord Byron 1788–1824
English poet

❦ Every year, in the fullness o' summer, when
the sukebind hangs heavy from the wains . . .
'tes the same. And when the spring comes
her hour is upon her again. 'Tes the hand of
Nature and we women cannot escape it.

Stella Gibbons 1902–89
English novelist
(from Cold Comfort Farm)

An absence, the decline of a dinner invitation, an unintentional coldness, can accomplish more than all the cosmetics and beautiful dresses in the world.

Marcel Proust 1871–1922
French novelist

There's no other [word] that's the right one, only one I am old-fashioned – it still shocks me a little. No, what shocks me is when a woman uses it and is not shocked at all until she realises I am. That's wrong too – what shocks is that all that magic, passion, excitement be summed up and dismissed in that one bald unlovely sound.

William Faulkner 1897–1962
American novelist

❦ When once a woman has given you her heart,
you can never get rid of the rest of her body.

Sir John Vanbrugh 1664–1726
English architect and playwright

❦ The perpetual hunger to be beautiful and
that thirst to be loved which is the real
curse of Eve.

Jean Rhys *c.* 1890–1979
British novelist and short-story writer

❦ 'Tisn't beauty, so to speak, nor good talk
necessarily. It's just It. Some women'll
stay in a man's memory if they once
walked down a street.

Rudyard Kipling 1865–1936
English writer and poet

❦ Beauty is all very well at first sight; but who ever looks at it when it has been in the house three days?

George Bernard Shaw 1856–1950
Irish playwright

❦ In matters of love men's eyes are always bigger than their bellies. They have violent appetites, 'tis true; but they have soon dined.

Sir John Vanbrugh 1664–1726
English architect and playwright

❦ There is no reciprocity. Men love women, women love children, children love hampsters.

Alice Thomas Ellis 1932—
English writer

❧ The heart prefers to move against the grain of circumstance; perversity is the soul's very life.

John Updike 1932—
American novelist and short-story writer

❧ So have I loitered my life away, reading books, looking at pictures, going to plays, hearing, thinking, writing on what pleased me best. I have wanted only one thing to make me happy, but wanting that have wanted everything.

William Hazlitt 1778–1830
English essayist

❧ Love's like the measles – all the worse when it comes late in life.

Douglas Jerrold 1803–57
English playwright and journalist

❦ The advantage of being married to an
   archaeologist is that the older you get, the
   more interested he becomes in you.

Agatha Christie 1890–1976
English writer of detective fiction

❦ Those who have some means think that the
   most important thing in the word is love. The
   poor know that it is money.

Gerald Brenan 1894–1987
British travel writer and novelist

❦ The poor cannot always reach those whom they
   want to love, and they can hardly ever escape
   from those whom they no longer love.

E. M. Forster 1879–1970
English novelist

❦ Mourning the loss of someone we love is
happiness compared with having to live with
someone we hate.

Jean de la Bruyère 1645–96
French writer

❦ Perfect fear casteth out love.

Cyril Connolly 1903–74
English writer

❦ If only it were possible to love without injury –
fidelity isn't enough . . . the hurt is in the act of
possession: we are too small in mind and body
to possess another person without pride or to
be possessed without humiliation.

Graham Greene 1904–91
English novelist

❧ Love is not looking in each other's eyes, but looking together in the same direction.

Antoine de Saint-Exupéry 1900–44
French novelist

❧ I always say I don't think everyone has the right to happiness or to be loved. Even the Americans have written into their constitution that you have the right to the 'pursuit of happiness'. You have the right to try but that is all.

Claire Rayner 1931—
English journalist

❧ Marriage is a bribe to make a housekeeper think she's a householder.

Thornton Wilder 1897–1975
American novelist and playwright

❦ The proper union of gin and vermouth is a great and sudden glory; it is one of the happiest marriages on earth, and one of the shortest lived.

Bernard De Voto 1897–1955
American writer

❦ If you find yourself unwilling to accept me, will you please pass this letter on to your sister Caroline.

Ralph, Lord Lovelace 1839–1906
English writer, alpinist and linguist
(proposal letter to Margaret Stuart Wortley)

❦ An unknown man in a lonely place is a permitted object of fear to a young woman privately bred.

Henry James 1843–1916
American novelist

❧ Human nature is so well disposed toward
those in interesting situations that a young
person who either marries or dies is sure
to be kindly spoken of.

Jane Austen 1775–1817
English novelist

❧ Take my word for it, the silliest woman can
manage a clever man; but it takes a very
clever woman to manage a fool.

Rudyard Kipling 1865–1936
English writer and poet

❧ Women have served all these centuries as
looking-glasses possessing the magic and
delicious power of reflecting the figure
of a man at twice its natural size.

Virginia Woolf 1882–1941
English novelist

❧ Marriage has many pains, but celibacy has no pleasures.

Samuel Johnson 1709–84
English poet, critic and lexicographer

❧ Marriage may often be a stormy lake, but celibacy is almost always a muddy horsepond.

Thomas Love Peacock 1785–1866
English novelist and poet

❧ If it were not for the presents, an elopement would be preferable.

George Ade 1866–1944
American humorist and playwright

❧ Whom God hath joined together no man ever shall put asunder: God will take care of that.

George Bernard Shaw 1856–1950
Irish playwright

❧ The critical period in matrimony is breakfast-time.

A. P. Herbert 1890–1971
English writer and humorist

❧ One disadvantage of being a hog is that at any moment some blundering fool may try to make a silk purse out of your wife's ear.

J. B. Morton ('Beachcomber') 1893–1975
British journalist

❧ My definition of marriage . . . it resembles a pair of shears, so joined that they cannot be separated; often moving in opposite directions, yet always punishing anyone who comes between them.

Sydney Smith 1771–1845
English clergyman and essayist

❦ A husband is what is left of a lover after the nerve has been extracted.

Helen Rowland 1875–1950
American writer

❦ In marriage, a man becomes slack and selfish, and undergoes a fatty degeneration of his moral being.

Robert Louis Stevenson 1850–94
Scottish novelist

❦ Medieval marriages were entirely a matter of property, and, as everyone knows, marriage without love means love without marriage.

Kenneth Clark 1903–83
English art historian

❧ Marriage is a wonderful invention; but, then again, so is a bicycle-repair kit.

Billy Connolly 1942—
Scottish comedian

❧ By god, D. H. Lawrence was right when he had said there must be a dumb, dark, dull, bitter belly-tension between a man and a woman, and how else could this be achieved save in the long monotony of marriage?

Stella Gibbons 1902–89
English novelist

❧ The deep, deep peace of the double-bed after the hurly-burly of the *chaise-longue*.

Mrs Patrick Campbell 1865–1940
English actress

❦ One doesn't have to get anywhere in a marriage.
It's not a public conveyance.

Iris Murdoch 1919–99
English novelist

❦ It was very good of God to let Carlyle and
Mrs Carlyle marry one another and
so make only two people miserable
instead of four.

Samuel Butler 1835–1902
English novelist

❦ I am not at all the sort of person you and
I took me for.

Jane Carlyle 1801–66
wife of Thomas Carlyle

❦ But a lifetime of happiness! No man alive
could bear it: it would be hell on earth.

George Bernard Shaw 1856–1950
Irish playwright

❦ I have never understood this liking for war.
It panders to instincts already catered for
within the scope of any respectable
domestic establishment.

Alan Bennett 1934—
English actor and playwright

❦ Sir, I have quarrelled with my wife; and a man
who has quarrelled with his wife is absolved
from all duty to his country.

Thomas Love Peacock 1785–1866
English novelist and poet
(from *Nightmare Abbey*)

❧ A man may pass through a barrage with less damage to his character than through a squabble with a nagging wife. Many domestic and commercial experiences leave blacker and more permanent marks on the soul than thrusting a bayonet through an enemy in a trench fight.

George Bernard Shaw 1856–1950
Irish playwright

❧ I am happy now that Charles calls on my bedchamber less frequently than of old. As it is, I now endure but two calls a week and when I hear his steps outside my door I lie down on my bed, close my eyes, open my legs, and think of England.

Lady Hillingdon 1857–1940

❧ I wish I could care what you do or where
you go but I can't . . . My dear, I don't
give a damn.

Margaret Mitchell 1900–49
American novelist
(from *Gone with the Wind*)

❧ Dora Greenfield left her husband because she
was afraid of him. She decided six months later
to return to him for the same reason.

Iris Murdoch 1919–99
English novelist
(from *The Bell*)

❧ Strange to say what delight we married people
have to see these poor fools decoyed into
our condition.

Samuel Pepys 1633–1703
English diarist

❦ Yes, it seems suitable that things like that
should go on in London . . . It is better taste
somehow that a man should be unfaithful to his
wife away from home.

Barbara Pym 1913–80
English novelist

❦ A lover without indiscretion is no lover at all.

Thomas Hardy 1840–1928
English novelist and poet

❦ There is sanctuary in reading, sanctuary in
formal society, in the company of old friends
and in the giving of officious help to strangers,
but there is no sanctuary in one bed from the
memory of another.

Cyril Connolly 1903–74
English writer

❧ If you cannot have your dear husband for a
comfort and a delight, for a breadwinner
and a crosspatch, for a sofa, chair or a
hot-water bottle, one can use him as
a Cross to be Borne.

Stevie Smith 1902–71
English poet and novelist

❧ Literature is mostly about having sex and
not much about having children. Life is
the other way round.

David Lodge 1935—
English novelist

❧ Familiarity breeds contempt – and children.

Mark Twain 1835–1910
American writer

❦ Contraceptives: What Protestants use on all
   conceivable occasions.

Anonymous

❦ Impotence and sodomy are socially OK but
   birth control is flagrantly middle-class.

Evelyn Waugh 1903–66
English novelist

❦ It is now quite lawful for a Catholic woman to
   avoid pregnancy by a resort to mathematics,
   though she is still forbidden to resort to
   physics and chemistry.

H. L. Mencken 1880–1956
American journalist and literary critic

❦ Protestant women may take the pill. Roman Catholic women must keep taking *The Tablet*.

Irene Thomas
British writer and broadcaster

❦ We want better reasons for having children than not knowing how to prevent them.

Dora Russell 1894–1986
English feminist

❦ Prostitution. Selling one's body to keep one's soul: this is the meaning of the sins that were forgiven to the woman because she loved much: one might say of most marriages that they were selling one's soul to keep one's body.

Compton Mackenzie 1883–1972
English novelist

❧ You can now see the Female Eunuch the world over . . . spreading herself wherever blue jeans and Coca-Cola may go. Wherever you see nail varnish, lipstick, brassieres and high heels, the Eunuch has set up her camp.

Germaine Greer 1939—
Australian feminist

❧ A woman without a man is like a fish without a bicycle.

Gloria Steinem 1934—
American journalist

❧ A woman can forgive a man for the harm he does her, but she can never forgive him for the sacrifices he makes on her account.

W. Somerset Maugham 1874–1965
English novelist

❧ A man in the house is worth two in the street.

Mae West 1892–1980
American film actress

❧ The orgasm has replaced the Cross as the focus
of longing and the image of fulfilment.

Malcolm Muggeridge 1903–90
British journalist

❧ My brain? It's my second favourite organ.

Woody Allen 1935—
American film director, writer and actor

❧ You can lead a horticulture, but you can't
make her think.

Dorothy Parker 1893–1967
American critic and humorist

❦ He said it was artificial respiration, but now I
find I am to have his child.

Anthony Burgess 1917–93
English novelist and critic

❦ If there's anything I hate in modern novels it is
this sex obsession, this pseudo-tough realism
in which every sexual depravity is intimately
dissected. It drags one straight back to
Jane Austen.

Noël Coward 1899–1973
English playwright and composer

❦ The expense is damnable, the pleasure
momentary and the position ludicrous.

Lord Chesterfield 1694–1773
English statesman, orator and man of letters

❧ It doesn't matter what you do in the bedroom as long as you don't do it in the street and frighten the horses.

Mrs Patrick Campbell 1865–1940
English actress

❧ That [sex] was the most fun I ever had without laughing.

Woody Allen 1935—
American film director, writer and actor

❧ I let go of her wrists, closed the door with my elbow and slid past her. It was like the first time. 'You ought to carry insurance on those,' I said.

Raymond Chandler 1888–1959
American writer of detective fiction

❧ I wasn't kissing her, I was just whispering
in her mouth.

Chico Marx 1891–1961
American film comedian

❧ Beware of loose women in tight skirts
and tight women in loose skirts.

Anonymous

❧ It's not the men in my life that counts –
it's the life in my men.

Mae West 1892–1980
American film actress

❦   KATH: Can he be present at the birth of his child? . . .

    ED: It's all any reasonable child can expect if the dad is present at the conception.

Joe Orton 1933–67
English playwright
(from *Entertaining Mr Sloane*)

❦ It serves me right for putting all my eggs in one bastard.

Dorothy Parker 1893–1967
American critic and humorist
(on her abortion)

❦ A fast word about oral contraception. I asked a girl to go to bed with me and she said no.

Woody Allen 1935—
American film director, writer and actor

❧ Don't give to lovers you will replace
   irreplaceable presents.

Logan Pearsall Smith 1865–1946
American-born British writer

❧ Your idea of fidelity is not having more
   than one man in bed at the same time.

Frederic Raphael 1931—
British novelist and screenwriter

❧ Is sex dirty? Only if it's done right.

Woody Allen 1935—
American film director, writer and actor

❧ I gave up screwing around a long time ago.
   I came to the conclusion that sex is a
   sublimation of the work instinct.

David Lodge 1935—
English novelist

❧ A woman will always sacrifice herself if you give her the opportunity. It is her favourite form of self-indulgence.

W. Somerset Maugham 1874–1965
English novelist

❧ Most women are not so young as they are painted.

Max Beerbohm 1872–1956
English critic, essayist and caricaturist

❧ Thirty-five is a very attractive age. London society is full of women of the very highest birth who have, of their own free choice, remained thirty-five for years.

Oscar Wilde 1854–1900
Anglo-Irish playwright and poet

❦ [Dancing is] a perpendicular expression of a horizontal desire.

George Bernard Shaw 1856–1950
Irish playwright

❦ 'Always be civil to the girls, you never know whom they may marry' – an aphorism which has saved many an English spinster from being treated like an Indian widow.

Nancy Mitford 1904–73
English writer

❦ So this gentleman said a girl with brains ought to do something with them besides think.

Anita Loos 1893–1981
American writer

❧ You don't know a woman until you have
   had a letter from her.

Ada Leverson 1865–1936
English novelist

❧ Arguing with a woman is like trying to fold the
   airmail edition of *The Times* in a high wind.

Lord Mancroft 1914–87
British Conservative politician

❧ Women do not find it difficult nowadays to
   behave like men, but they often find it
   extremely difficult to behave like gentlemen.

Compton Mackenzie 1883–1972
English novelist

❦ The stereotype is the Eternal Feminine. She is
   the Sexual Object sought by all men, and by
   all women. She is of neither sex, for she has
   herself no sex at all. Her value is solely
   attested by the demand she excites in others.
   All she must contribute is her existence.
   She need achieve nothing, for she is
   the reward of achievement.

Germaine Greer 1939—
Australian feminist

❦ Don't knock masturbation. It's sex with
   someone I love.

Woody Allen 1935—
American film director, writer and actor

❦ He fell in love with himself at first sight and
it is a passion to which he has always
remained faithful.

Anthony Powell 1905–2000
English novelist

❦ He who is in love with himself has at least this
advantage – he won't encounter many rivals in
his love.

Lichtenberg

❦ There, standing at the piano, was the original
good time who had been had by all.

Kenneth Tynan 1927–80
English theatre critic

❦ On bisexuality: It immediately doubles your chances of a date on a Saturday night.

Woody Allen 1935—
American film director, writer and actor

❦ I'm all for bringing back the birch, but only between consenting adults.

Gore Vidal 1925—
American novelist and critic

❦ My dear fellow, buggers can't be choosers.

Maurice Bowra 1898–1971
English scholar and literary critic
(on being told he should not marry
anyone as plain as his fiancée)

Soup at Luncheon

❦   Gentlemen do not take soup at luncheon.

Lord Curzon 1859–1925
British Conservative politician

❦   I ask very little. Some fragments of
    Pamphilides, a Choctaw blood-mask, the
    prose of Scaliger the Elder, a painting by
    Fuseli, an occasional visit to the all-in
    wrestling or to my meretrix; a cook
    who can produce a passable *poulet à la
    Khmer*, a Pong vase. Simple tastes, you
    will agree, and it is my simple habit to
    indulge them.

Cyril Connolly 1903–74
English writer

❦ Good God, do you mean to say this place is a club?

F. E. Smith 1872–1930
British Conservative politician and lawyer
(on being approached by the secretary of the Athenaeum,
which he had been in the habit of using as a
convenience on the way to his office)

❦ I thought everyone must know that a short jacket is always worn with a silk hat at a private view in the morning.

Edward VII 1841–1910

❦ The sense of being well-dressed gives a feeling of inward tranquillity which religion is powerless to bestow.

Miss C. F. Forbes 1817–1911
English writer

❦ The only infallible rule we know is that the man who is always talking about being a gentleman never is one.

R. S. Surtees 1805–64
English sporting journalist and novelist

❦ There are, it is true, still a few minor points of life which may serve to demarcate the upper class, but they are only minor ones . . . when drunk, gentlemen often become amorous or maudlin or vomit in public, but they never become truculent.

Alan S. C. Ross 1907–80
British linguistics scholar

It is almost a definition of a gentleman to say
that he is one who never inflicts pain.

John Henry Newman 1801–90
English theologian

Let the scintillations of your wit be like the
coruscations of summer lightning, lambent but
innocuous.

Edward Meyrick Goulburn 1818–97
Dean of Norwich

It is a secret in the Oxford sense. You may
tell it to only one person at a time.

Lord Franks 1905–1992
British philosopher and administrator

❧ Sir, there is no settling the point of precedency between a louse and a flea.

Samuel Johnson 1709–84
English poet, critic and lexicographer

❧ You can be in the Horseguards and still be common, dear.

Terence Rattigan 1911–77
English playwright

❧ Ladies were ladies in those days; they did not do things themselves.

Gwen Raverat 1885–1957
English wood-engraver

❧ The young ladies entered the drawing-room in the full fervour of sisterly animosity.

R. S. Surtees 1805–64
English sporting journalist and novelist

❦ She experienced all the cosiness and irritation
which can come from living with thoroughly
nice people with whom one has nothing
in common.

Barbara Pym 1913–80
English novelist

❦ I have, all my life long, been lying till noon;
yet I tell all young men, and tell them with
great sincerity, that nobody who does not
rise early will ever do any good.

Samuel Johnson 1709–84
English poet, critic and lexicographer

❦ Economy was always 'elegant', and money-spending always 'vulgar' and ostentatious – a sort of sour-grapeism, which made us very peaceful and satisfied.

Elizabeth Gaskell 1810–65
English novelist

❦ All decent people live beyond their incomes nowadays, and those who aren't respectable live beyond other people's.

Saki (Hector Hugh Munro) 1870–1916
Scottish writer

❦ He was a gentleman who was generally spoken of as having nothing a year, paid quarterly.

R. S. Surtees 1805–64
English sporting journalist and novelist

❧ The Victorians had not been anxious to go away
   for the weekend. The Edwardians, on the
   contrary, were nomadic.

T. H. White 1906–64
English novelist

❧ Gentlemen know that fresh air should be kept
   in its proper place – out of doors – and that,
   God having given us indoors and out-of-doors,
   we should not attempt to do away with this
   distinction.

Rose Macaulay 1881–1958
English novelist

❧ I have no relish for the country; it is a kind of
   healthy grave.

Sydney Smith 1771–1845
English clergyman and essayist

❦ My living in Yorkshire was so far out of the way that it was actually twelve miles from a lemon.

Sydney Smith 1771–1845
English clergyman and essayist

❦ Anybody can be good in the country.

Oscar Wilde 1854–1900
Anglo-Irish playwright and poet

❦ It is my belief, Watson, founded upon my experience, that the lowest and vilest alleys in London do not present a more dreadful record of sin than does the smiling and beautiful countryside.

Sir Arthur Conan Doyle 1859–1930
Scottish-born writer of detective fiction

❧ But if he does really think that there is no
distinction between virtue and vice, why,
sir, when he leaves our houses, let us
count our spoons.

Samuel Johnson 1709–84
English poet, critic and lexicographer

❧ The art of hospitality is to make guests feel at
home when you wish they were.

Anonymous

❧ You must come again when you have less time.

Walter Sickert 1860–1942
German-born British artist

❧ To find a friend one must close one eye.
To keep him – two.

Norman Douglas 1868–1952
Scottish-born novelist and essayist

❧ How few of his friends' houses would a man choose to be at when he is sick.

Samuel Johnson 1709–84
English poet, critic and lexicographer

❧ The best thing we can do is to make wherever we're lost in look as much like home as we can.

Christopher Fry 1907—
English playwright

❧ Good breeding consists in concealing how much we think of ourselves and how little we think of the other person.

Mark Twain 1835–1910
American writer

❦ If a man does not make new acquaintance as
  he advances through life, he will soon find
  himself left alone. A man, sir, should keep
  his friendship in constant repair.

Samuel Johnson 1709–84
English poet, critic and lexicographer

❦ If you want to discover your true opinion of
  anybody, observe the impression made on
  you by the first sight of a letter from him.

Artur Schopenhauer 1788–1860
German philosopher

❦ Talking is often a torment to me. I need days of
  silence to recover from the futility of words.

Carl Gustav Jung 1875–1961
Swiss psychologist

❦ My life is spent in a perpetual alternation
between two rhythms, the rhythm of
attracting people for fear I may be lonely,
and the rhythm of trying to get rid of them
because I know that I am bored.

C. E. M. Joad 1891–1953
English philosopher

❦ A little sincerity is a dangerous thing, and a
great deal of it is absolutely fatal.

Oscar Wilde 1854–1900
Anglo-Irish playwright and poet

❦ A man is in general better pleased when he
has a good dinner upon his table than
when his wife talks Greek.

Samuel Johnson 1709–84
English poet, critic and lexicographer

❦ Always, sir, set a high value on spontaneous
kindness. He whose inclination prompts him
to cultivate your friendship of his own accord,
will love you more than one whom you have
been at pains to attach to you.

Samuel Johnson 1709–84
English poet, critic and lexicographer

❦ As a host at his breakfast parties, although
lacking the essential grace and fragility of an
eighteenth-century *marquise*, being as a rule
unshaven and clad in insecure, egg-stained
pyjamas, he managed in his own harum-scarum
way to evoke a certain 'salon' spirit.

Noël Coward 1899–1973
English playwright, actor and composer
(of Alexander Woollcott)

❧ I'm a man more dined against than dining.

Maurice Bowra 1898–1971
English scholar and literary critic

❧ Dinner at the Huntercombes' possessed only
two dramatic features – the wine was a farce
and the food a tragedy.

Anthony Powell 1905–2000
English novelist

❧ You are offered a piece of bread and butter that
feels like a damp handkerchief and sometimes,
when cucumber is added to it, like a wet one.

Compton Mackenzie 1883–1972
English novelist

❦ A cucumber should be well sliced, and
   dressed with pepper and vinegar, and
   then thrown out, as good for nothing.

Samuel Johnson 1709–84
English poet, critic and lexicographer

❦ Fish, to taste right, must swim three times –
   in water, in butter, and in wine.

Polish proverb

❦ Let the salad-maker be a spendthrift for oil,
   a miser for vinegar, a statesman for salt
   and a madman for mixing.

Spanish proverb

.

182

❧ And now with some pleasure I find that it's seven; and must cook dinner. Haddock and sausage meat. I think it is true that one gains a certain hold on sausage and haddock by writing them down.

Virginia Woolf 1882–1941
English novelist

❧ The best number for a dinner party is two – myself and a dam' good head waiter.

Nubar Gulbenkian 1896–1972
British industrialist and philanthropist

❧ We each day dig our graves with our teeth.

Samuel Smiles 1812–1904
English writer

❧ Mr Leopold Bloom ate with relish the inner
organs of beasts and fowls. He liked thick
giblet soup, nutty gizzards, a stuffed roast
heart, liverslices fried with crustcrumbs, fried
hencod's roes. Most of all he liked grilled
mutton kidneys which gave to his palate
a fine tang of faintly scented urine.

James Joyce 1882–1941
Irish novelist
(from *Ulysses*)

❧ The tumult and the shouting dies,
The captains and the kings depart,
And we are left with large supplies
Of cold blancmange and rhubarb tart.

Ronald Knox 1888–1957
English writer and Roman Catholic priest

❦ And the sooner the tea's out of the way,
the sooner we can get out the gin, eh?

Henry Reed 1914–86
English poet and playwright

❦ Alcohol is a very necessary article . . . It makes
life bearable to millions of people who could
not endure their existence if they were quite
sober. It enables Parliament to do things at
eleven at night that no sane person would
do at eleven in the morning.

George Bernard Shaw 1856–1950
Irish playwright

❦ A man shouldn't fool with booze until he's fifty;
then he's a damn fool if he doesn't.

William Faulkner 1897–1962
American novelist

❦ Some weasel took the cork out of my lunch.

W. C. Fields 1880–1946
American humorist

❦ It was my Uncle George who discovered
that alcohol was a food well in advance
of medical thought.

P. G. Wodehouse 1881–1975
English writer

❦ I have taken more out of alcohol than alcohol
has taken out of me.

Winston Churchill 1874–1965
British Conservative politician

❦ At the present moment, the whole Fleet's
 lit up. When I say 'lit up', I mean lit up
 by fairy lamps.

Thomas Woodroofe 1899–1978
British naval officer

❦ I'm really not much of a drinker,
 Just 1 or 2 at the most.
 With 3 I'm under the table,
 With 4 I'm under my host.

Dorothy Parker 1893–1967
American critic and humorist

❦ But I'm not so think as you drunk I am.

J. C. Squire 1884–1958
English man of letters

❦ R–E–M–O–R–S–E!
Those dry Martinis did the work for me;
Last night at twelve I felt immense,
Today I feel like thirty cents.
My eyes are bleared, my coppers hot,
I'll try to eat, but I cannot.
It is no time for mirth and laughter,
The cold, grey dawn of the morning after.

George Ade 1866–1944
American humorist and playwright

❦ Many a man who thinks to found a home
discovers that he has merely opened a
tavern for his friends.

Norman Douglas 1868–1952
Scottish-born novelist and essayist

A hardened and shameless tea-drinker, who
has for twenty years diluted his meals with
only the infusion of this fascinating plant;
whose kettle has scarcely time to cool; who
with tea amuses the evening, with tea
solaces the midnight, and with tea
welcomes the morning.

Samuel Johnson 1709–84
English poet, critic and lexicographer

A good cigar is as great a comfort to a man
as a good cry is to a woman.

Edward George Bulwer-Lytton 1803–73
English politician and man of letters

❦ A custom loathsome to the eye, hateful to the
nose, harmful to the brain, dangerous to the
lungs, and in the black, stinking fume
thereof, nearest resembling the horrible
Stygian smoke of the pit that is bottomless . . .

James I (James VI of Scotland) 1566–1625
(from *A Counterblast to Tobacco*)

❦ Herein is not only a great vanity, but a great
contempt of God's good gifts, that the
sweetness of man's breath, being a good gift of
God, should be wilfully corrupted by this
stinking smoke.

James I (James VI of Scotland) 1566–1625
(from *A Counterblast to Tobacco*)

❦ All the things I really like to do are either illegal, immoral or fattening.

Alexander Woollcott 1887–1943
American writer

❦ When you don't have any money, the problem is food. When you have money, it's sex. When you have both it's health.

J. P. Donleavy 1926—
Irish-American novelist

Goodbye, Moralitee!

❧ As my poor father used to say
In 1863,
Once people start on all this Art,
Goodbye, moralitee!

A. P. Herbert 1890–1971
English writer and humorist

❧ It is through Art, and through Art only, that
we can realise our perfection; through Art,
and through Art only, that we can shield
ourselves from the sordid perils of
actual existence.

Oscar Wilde 1854–1900
Anglo-Irish playwright and poet

❧ There is no more sombre enemy of good art
than the pram in the hall.

Cyril Connolly 1903–74
English writer

❦ Could we teach taste or genius by rules,
   they would be no longer taste and genius.

Joshua Reynolds 1723–92
English painter

❦ Real culture lives by sympathies and
   admirations, not by dislikes and disdains –
   under all misleading wrappings it pounces
   unerringly upon the human core.

William James 1842–1910
American philosopher

❦ Whom the gods wish to destroy they
   first call promising.

Cyril Connolly 1903–74
English writer

❦ I have seen, and heard, much of Cockney impudence before now; but never expected to hear a coxcomb ask two hundred guineas for flinging a pot of paint in the public's face.

> John Ruskin 1819–1900
> English art and social critic
> (on Whistler's *Nocturne in Black and Gold*)

❦ Nothing knits man to man, the Manchester School wisely taught, like the frequent passage from hand to hand of cash.

> Walter Sickert 1860–1942
> English painter

❦ No. I ask it for the knowledge of a lifetime.

> James McNeill Whistler 1834–1903
> American-born painter
> (in his case against Ruskin, replying to the question,
> 'For two days' labour, you ask two hundred guineas?')

❦ The mind is but a barren soil; a soil which is
   soon exhausted, and will produce no crop,
   or only one, unless it be continually
   fertilised and enriched with foreign matter.

Joshua Reynolds 1723–92
English painter

❦ A product of the untalented, sold by the
   unprincipled to the utterly bewildered.

Al Capp 1907–79
American cartoonist
(on abstract art)

❦ All that I desire to point out is the general
   principle that Life imitates Art far more
   than Art imitates Life.

Oscar Wilde 1854–1900
Anglo-Irish playwright and poet

❦ Do not judge this movement kindly. It is not just another amusing stunt. It is defiant – the desperate act of men too profoundly convinced of the rottenness of our civilisation to want to save a shred of its respectability.

Sir Herbert Read 1893–1968
English art historian
(on the Surrealist Movement)

❦ If Botticelli were alive today he'd be working for *Vogue*.

Peter Ustinov 1921—
Russian-born actor, director and writer

❦ I maintain that two and two would continue to make four, in spite of the whine of the amateur for three, or the cry of the critic for five.

James McNeill Whistler 1834–1903
American-born painter
(Whistler v. Ruskin)

❦ Why don't they stick to murder and leave
   art to us?

Jacob Epstein 1880–1959
British sculptor
(on hearing that his statue of Lazarus in New College
chapel, Oxford, kept Khrushchev awake at night)

❦ Few have heard of Fra Luca Pacioli, the
   inventor of double-entry book-keeping;
   but he has probably had much more influence
   on human life than has Dante or Michelangelo.

Herbert J. Muller 1890–1967

❦ Architecture is the art of how to waste space.

Philip Johnson 1906—
American architect

❧ Sir Christopher Wren
Said, 'I am going to dine with some men.
If anybody calls
Say I am designing St Paul's.'

Edmund Clerihew Bentley 1875–1956
English writer

❧ All over the country the latest and most
scientific methods of mass-production are
being utilised to turn out a stream of old oak
beams, leaded window-panes and small discs
of bottle-glass, all structural devices which our
ancestors lost no time in abandoning as soon
as an increase in wealth and knowledge
enabled them to do so.

Sir Osbert Lancaster 1908–86
English writer and cartoonist

❦ Remember that the most beautiful things
in the world are the most useless;
peacocks and lilies for instance.

John Ruskin 1819–1900
English art and social critic

❦ Have nothing in your houses that you do not
know to be useful, or believe to be beautiful.

William Morris 1834–96
English writer, artist and designer

❦ Fan-vaulting . . . from an aesthetic standpoint
frequently belongs to the 'Last-Supper-carved-
on-a-peachstone' class of masterpiece.

Sir Osbert Lancaster 1908–86
English writer and cartoonist

❧ Alas, for our towns and cities! Monstrous carbuncles of concrete have erupted in gentle Georgian squares.

Raine, Countess Spencer 1929—

❧ A monstrous carbuncle on the face of a much-loved and elegant friend.

Prince Charles 1948—
(on the proposed extension to the
National Gallery, London)

❧ All this talk of art is dangerous; it brings the ears so forward that they act as blinkers.

Edwin Lutyens 1869–1944
English architect

❦ I hope I may die before you, so that I may see
Heaven before you improve it.

Anonymous
(a remark made to Capability Brown)

❦ Nymphs and tribal deities of excessive female
physique and alarming size balanced
precariously on broken pediments, threatening
the passer-by with a shower of stone fruit.

Sir Osbert Lancaster 1908–86
English writer and cartoonist

❦ Radio and television . . . have succeeded in
lifting the manufacture of banality out of
the sphere of handicraft and placing it
in that of a major industry.

Nathalie Sarraute 1902–99
French novelist

❦ The media. It sounds like a convention
of spiritualists.

Tom Stoppard 1937—
British playwright

❦ Why should people go out and pay to see bad
movies when they can stay at home and see bad
television for nothing?

Sam Goldwyn 1882–1974
American film producer

❦ Television has brought back murder into the
home – where it belongs.

Alfred Hitchcock 1899–1980
British-born film director

❦ I wouldn't say when you've seen one Western you've seen the lot; but when you've seen the lot you get the feeling you've seen one.

Katharine Whitehorn 1926—
English journalist

❦ Hollywood money isn't money. It's congealed snow – melts in your hand, and there you are.

Dorothy Parker 1893–1967
American critic and humorist

❦ A trip through a sewer in a glass-bottomed boat.

Wilson Mizner 1876–1933
American playwright
(of Hollywood)

❦ That's the way with these directors, they're
   always biting the hand that lays the golden egg.

   Sam Goldwyn 1882–1974
   American film producer

❦ I reflected gleefully that for five hundred dollars
   I would gladly consider turning *War and Peace*
   into a music-hall sketch.

   Noël Coward 1899–1973
   English playwright, actor and composer

❦ Pictures are for entertainment, messages
   should be delivered by Western Union.

   Sam Goldwyn 1882–1974
   American film producer

❧ The historian, essentially, wants more
documents than he can really use; the
dramatist only wants more liberties than
he can really take.

Henry James 1843–1916
American novelist

❧ Damn them! They will not let my play run,
but they steal my thunder!

John Dennis 1657–1734
English critic, poet and playwright
(on hearing his new thunder effects
used at a performance of *Macbeth*)

❧ Acting is a masochistic form of exhibitionism.
It is not quite the occupation of an adult.

Laurence Olivier 1907–89
English actor and director

❧ My dear boy, forget about motivation. Just say
the lines and don't trip over the furniture.

Noël Coward 1899–1973
English playwright, actor and composer

❧ Being a star has made it possible for me to get
insulted in places where the average negro
could never hope to go and get insulted.

Sammy Davis Jnr 1925–90
American entertainer

❧ The weasel under the cocktail cabinet.

Harold Pinter 1930—
English playwright
(on being asked
what his plays were about)

❦ Since the war a terrible pall of significance has fallen over plays.

Noël Coward 1899–1973
English playwright, actor and composer

❦ I prefer Offenbach to Bach often.

Sir Thomas Beecham 1879–1961
English conductor

❦ Rock journalism is people who can't write interviewing people who can't talk for people who can't read.

Frank Zappa 1940–93
American rock musician and songwriter

The Itch
of Literature

❧ When once the itch of literature comes over
a man, nothing can cure it but the
scratching of a pen.

Samuel Lover 1797–1868
Irish writer

❧ The writer's only responsibility is to his art.
He will be completely ruthless if he is a good
one. He has a dream. It anguishes him so
much he must get rid of it. He has no peace
until then. Everything goes by the board . . .
If a writer has to rob his mother, he will not
hesitate; the 'Ode on a Grecian Urn' is
worth any number of old ladies.

William Faulkner 1897–1962
American novelist

The business of the poet and novelist is to show the sorriness underlying the grandest things, and the grandeur underlying the sorriest things.

Thomas Hardy 1840–1928
English novelist and poet

Well! It is now public, and you will stand for your privileges, we know: to read, and censure. Do so, but buy it first. That doth best commend a book, the stationer says.

John Heming 1556–1630 and Henry Condell d. 1627
(joint editors of the First Folio Shakespeare)

Shakespeare – the nearest thing in incarnation to the eye of God.

Laurence Olivier 1907–89
English actor and director

❧ It must be at last confessed that as we owe
everything to him [Shakespeare], he owes
something to us; that, if much of our praise is
paid by perception and judgement, much is
likewise given by custom and veneration. We fix
our eyes upon his graces, and turn them from
his deformities, and endure in him what we
should in another loathe or despise.

Samuel Johnson 1709–84
English poet, critic and lexicographer

❧ When I read Shakespeare I am struck with
                                    wonder
That such trivial people should must and
                                    thunder
In such lovely language.

D. H. Lawrence 1885–1930
English novelist and poet

❦ Who, as he was a happy imitator of Nature,
   was a most gentle expresser of it. His mind
   and hand went together: and what he
   thought, he uttered with that easiness that
   we have scarce received from him a blot.

John Heming 1556–1630 and Henry Condell d. 1627
(joint editors of the First Folio Shakespeare)

❦ He that tries to recommend him [Shakespeare]
   by select quotations, will succeed like the
   pedant in Hierocles, who, when he offered
   his house to sale, carried a brick in his
   pocket as a specimen.

Samuel Johnson 1709–84
English poet, critic and lexicographer

❦ The blockheads talk of my being like
Shakespeare – not fit to tie his brogues.

Walter Scott 1771–1832
Scottish novelist and poet

❦ To fight with form, to wrestle and to rage
Till at the last upon the conquered page
The shadows of created beauty fall.

Lord Alfred Douglas 1870–1945
English poet

❦ Every true lover of poetry knows that when he
cites great lines it is not the poetry but the
hearer that is to be judged.

Coventry Patmore 1823–96
English poet

❦ All books are either dreams or swords,
   You can cut, or you can drug, with words.

> Amy Lowell 1874–1925
> American poet

❦ The pen, in our age, weighs heavier in the social
   scale than the sword of a Norman baron.

> G. H. Lewes 1817–78
> English man of letters

❦ It is hard for a woman to define her feelings
   in language which is chiefly made by men
   to express theirs.

> Thomas Hardy 1840–1928
> English novelist and poet

❦   This is an important book, the critic assumes,
    because it deals with war. This is an
    insignificant book because it deals with
    the feelings of women in a drawing-room.

Virginia Woolf 1882–1941
English novelist

❦   Your borrowers of books – those mutilators
    of collections, spoilers of the symmetry of
    shelves and creators of odd volumes.

Charles Lamb 1775–1834
English writer

❦   If you file your wastepaper basket for fifty years,
    you have a public library.

Tony Benn 1925—
British Labour politician

❦ A library is thought in cold storage.

Lord Samuel 1870–1963
British Liberal politician

❦ When I am dead, I hope it may be said: 'His sins were scarlet, but his books were read.'

Hilaire Belloc 1870–1953
French-born British writer and poet

❦ A writer's ambition should be . . . to trade a hundred contemporary readers for ten readers in ten years' time and for one reader in a hundred years.

Arthur Koestler 1905–83
Hungarian-born writer

❦ If my books had been any worse, I should
not have been invited to Hollywood, and
if they had been any better, I should
not have come.

Raymond Chandler 1888–1959
American writer of detective fiction

❦ Writing is not a profession but a vocation
of unhappiness.

Georges Simenon 1903–89
Belgian novelist

❦ I hate the sort of licence that English people
give themselves . . . to spread over and flop
and roll about. I feel as fastidious as
though I wrote with acid.

Katherine Mansfield 1888–1923
New Zealand-born short-story writer

❧ You who scribble, yet hate all who write . . .
   And with faint praises one another damn.

William Wycherley c. 1640–1716
English playwright

❧ It took me fifteen years to discover that I
   had no talent for writing, but I couldn't
   give it up because by that time I was
   too famous.

Robert Benchley 1889–1945
American humorist

❧ The best fame is a writer's fame: it's enough
   to get you a table at a good restaurant, but not
   enough to get you interrupted when you eat.

Fran Lebowitz 1946—
American humorous writer

❦ My English text is chaste, and all licentious
passages are left in the obscurity of a
learned language.

Edward Gibbon 1737–94
English historian

❦ The great tragedy of the classical languages
is to have been born twins.

Geoffrey Madan 1895–1947
English bibliophile

❦ He [Winston Churchill] mobilized the English
language and sent it into battle to steady his
fellow countrymen and hearten those
Europeans upon whom the long dark
night of tyranny had descended.

Ed Murrow 1908–65
American broadcaster and journalist

❧ It is a terrible alternative that an author must
either starve and be esteemed, or be vilified
and get money.

Fanny Burney 1752–1840
English novelist and diarist

❧ Deprivation is for me what daffodils were
for Wordsworth.

Philip Larkin 1922–85
English poet

❧ It is burning a farthing candle at Dover
to show light at Calais.

Samuel Johnson 1709–84
English poet, critic and lexicographer
(on Thomas Sheridan's influence on the English language)

❧ To my daughter Leonora without whose
never-failing sympathy and encouragement
this book would have been finished in
half the time.

P. G. Wodehouse 1881–1975
English writer

❧ All the characters in this book are entirely
fictitious, and any person claiming to be
any one of them will be prosecuted.

Author's note in a book

❧ Every drop of ink in my pen ran cold.

Horace Walpole 1717–97
English writer and connoisseur

❦ The virtue of much literature is that it is
   dangerous and may do you extreme harm.

   John Mortimer 1923—
   English novelist, barrister and playwright

❦ The vocabulary of *Bradshaw* is nervous and
   terse, but limited. The selection of words
   would hardly lend itself to the sending
   of general messages.

   Sir Arthur Conan Doyle 1859–1930
   Scottish- born writer of detective fiction

❦ There's a hell of a distance between
   wisecracking and wit. Wit has truth in it;
   wisecracking is simply callisthenics with words.

   Dorothy Parker 1893–1967
   American critic and humorist

❧ Literature is strewn with the wreckage of
men who have minded beyond reason
the opinion of others.

Virginia Woolf 1882–1941
English novelist

❧ An autobiography is an obituary in serial
form with the last instalment missing.

Quentin Crisp 1908–99
English writer

❧ The past exudes legend: one can't make pure
clay of time's mud. There is no life that can
be recaptured wholly; as it was. Which is
to say that all biography is ultimately fiction.

Bernard Malamud 1914–86
American novelist and short-story writer

❧ Every great man nowadays has his disciples, and it is always Judas who writes the biography.

Oscar Wilde 1854–1900
Anglo-Irish playwright and poet

❧ Discretion is not the better part of biography.

Lytton Strachey 1880–1932
English biographer

❧ History repeats itself. Historians repeat each other.

Philip Guedalla 1889–1944
British historian and biographer

❧ Ignorance is the first requisite of the historian –
ignorance, which simplifies and clarifies,
which selects and omits, with a placid
perfection unattainable by the highest art.

Lytton Strachey 1880–1932
English biographer

❧ Great and good is the typical don, and of
                    evil and wrong the foe.
Good, and great, I'm a don myself, and
                    therefore I ought to know.

A. D. Godley 1856–1925
English classicist

❧ Don's room, like the nest of a foolish bird.

Geoffrey Madan 1895–1947
English bibliophile

❦ The llama is a woolly sort of fleecy hairy goat,
With an indolent expression and an
                              undulating throat
Like an unsuccessful literary man.

Hilaire Belloc 1870–1953
French-born British writer and poet

❦ It is better to read trash with enjoyment than
masterpieces with yawing groans.

Harold Nicolson 1886–1968
British diplomat, author and critic

❦ A man ought to read just as inclination leads
him; for what he reads as a task will do him
little good.

Samuel Johnson 1709–84
English poet, critic and lexicographer

❦   I never read a book before reviewing it;
    it prejudices a man so.

Sydney Smith 1771–1845
English clergyman and essayist

❦   Reading isn't an occupation we encourage
    among police officers. We try to keep the paper
    work down to a minimum.

Joe Orton 1933–67
English playwright

❦   Is it a book you would even wish your wife or
    your servants to read?

Mervyn Griffith-Jones 1909–79
British lawyer
(of D. H. Lawrence's *Lady Chatterley's Lover*)

❦ King David and King Solomon
   Led merry, merry lives,
   With many, many lady friends,
   And many, many wives;
   But when old age crept over them –
   With many, many qualms! –
   King Solomon wrote the Proverbs
   And King David wrote the Psalms.

James Ball Naylor 1860–1945

❦ Literature is the orchestration of platitudes.

Thornton Wilder 1897–1975
American novelist and playwright

❦ If you steal from one author, it's plagiarism;
   if you steal from many, it's research.

Wilson Mizner 1876–1933
American playwright

❦ Plagiarize! Let no one else's work evade your eyes,
    Remember why the good Lord made your eyes.

Tom Lehrer 1928—
American humorist

❦ Misquotation is, in fact, the pride and privilege
    of the learned. A widely read man never
    quotes accurately, for the rather obvious
    reason that he has read too widely.

Hesketh Pearson 1887–1964
English actor and biographer

❦ Clear writers, like clear fountains, do not
    seem so deep as they are; the turbid
    look the most profound.

Walter Savage Landor 1775–1864
English poet

❦ Each equation . . . in the book would
   halve the sales.

Stephen Hawking 1942—
English theoretical physicist

❦ The shelf life of the modern hardback writer
   is somewhere between the milk and the
   yoghurt.

Calvin Trillin

❦ Beware of women – they always have a
   manuscript hidden about their person.

Logan Pearsall Smith 1865–1946
American-born British writer

❧ As artists they're rot, but as providers they're oil wells; they gush.

Dorothy Parker 1893–1967
American critic and humorist
(on lady novelists)

❧ After being turned down by numerous publishers, he had decided to write for posterity.

George Ade 1866–1944
American humorist and playwright

❧ Being published by the Oxford University Press is rather like being married to a duchess: the honour is almost greater than the pleasure.

G. M. Young 1882–1959
English historical essayist

❧ 'Feather-footed through the plashy fen passes
the questing vole' . . . 'Yes,' said the managing
editor. 'That must be good style.'

Evelyn Waugh 1903–66
English novelist
(from *Scoop*)

❧ I will not go down to posterity talking
bad grammar.

Benjamin Disraeli 1804–81
British Conservative politician and novelist
(while correcting proofs of his last parliamentary speech)

❧ This is the sort of English up with which I
will not put.

Winston Churchill 1874–1965
British Conservative politician

❧ Would you convey my compliments to the
purist who reads your proofs and tell him or her
that I write in a sort of broken-down patois
which is something like the way a Swiss waiter
talks, and that when I split an infinitive, God
damn it, I split it so it will stay split.

Raymond Chandler 1888–1959
American writer of detective fiction

❧ Behind many an initially mediocre but
ultimately fêted male author slumps a
long-suffering rarely acknowledged
woman copy-editor.

Katy Cooper
(in a letter to the *Guardian*)

❧ It is dangerous to have any intercourse or dealings with small authors. They are as troublesome to handle, as easy to discompose, as difficult to pacify, and leave as unpleasant marks on you, as children.

Walter Savage Landor 1775–1864
English poet

❧ Of all the literary scenes
Saddest this sight to me:
The graves of little magazines
Who died to make verse free.

Keith Preston 1884–1927
American poet

❦ The next Augustan age will dawn on the other side of the Atlantic. There will, perhaps, be a Thucydides at Boston, a Xenophon at New York and, in time, a Virgil at Mexico and a Newton at Peru. At last, some curious traveller from Lima will visit England and give a description of the ruins of St Paul's, like the editions of Balbec and Palmyra.

Horace Walpole 1717–97
English writer and connoisseur

Come and Sit
by Me

❦   If you have nothing good to say about anyone,
    come and sit by me.

Alice Roosevelt Longworth

❦   Impropriety is the soul of wit.

W. Somerset Maugham 1874–1965
English novelist

❦   What is merit? The opinion one man entertains
    of another.

Lord Palmerston 1784–1865
British politician

❦ The verses, when they were written, resembled
nothing so much as spoonfuls of boiling oil,
ladled out by a fiendish monkey at an upstairs
window upon such passers-by whom the wretch
had a grudge against.

Lytton Stratchey 1880–1932
English biographer

❦ A very weak-minded fellow, I am afraid, and,
like a feather pillow, bears the marks of
the last person who sat on him!

Earl Haig 1861–1928
(describing the 17th Earl of Derby)

❦ He's so wet you could shoot snipe off him.

Anthony Powell 1905–2000
English novelist

❧ A doormat in a world of boots.

Jean Rhys *c.*1890–1979
British novelist and short-story writer

❧ We are nauseated by the sight of trivial
personalities decomposing in the
eternity of print.

Virginia Woolf 1882–1941
English novelist

❧ Dr Donne's verses are like the peace of God;
they pass all understanding.

James I (James VI of Scotland) 1566–1625

❧ One of the greatest geniuses that ever existed,
Shakespeare, undoubtedly wanted taste.

Horace Walpole 1717–97
English writer and connoisseur

❦ Thank you, madam, the agony is abated.

Thomas Babington, 1st Baron Macaulay 1800–59
English politician and historian
(aged four, having had hot coffee spilt over his legs)

❦ He [Macaulay] has occasional flashes of silence
that make his conversation perfectly delightful.

Sydney Smith 1771–1845
English clergyman and essayist

❦ He sipped at a weak hock and seltzer
As he gazed at the London skies
Through the Nottingham lace of the curtains
Or was it his bees-winged eyes?

John Betjeman 1906–84
English poet
(of Oscar Wilde)

❦ If, with the literate, I am
    Impelled to try an epigram,
    I never seek to take the credit;
    We all assume that Oscar said it.

Dorothy Parker 1893–1967
American critic and humorist

❦ 'My dear Sphinx, I walk about all day with a
    beautiful young man with a knife in his hand.'
    'My dear Oscar, I'm sure he has a fork in his
    other hand.'

Oscar Wilde (1854–1900)
to Ada Leverson (1865–1936)

❦ He seemed at ease and to have the look of the
    last gentleman in Europe.

Ada Leverson 1865–1936
English novelist
(of Oscar Wilde)

❦　It is leviathan retrieving pebbles. It is a
magnificent but painful hippopotamus
resolved at any cost, even at the cost of its
dignity, upon picking up a pea which has
got into a corner of its den.

H. G. Wells 1866–1946
English novelist
(of Henry James)

❦　The work of Henry James has always seemed
divisible by a simple dynastic arrangement
into three reigns: James I, James II and
the Old Pretender.

Philip Guedalla 1889–1944
British historian and biographer

🐛 Poor Henry [James], he's spending eternity wandering round and round a stately park and the fence is just too high for him to peep over and they're having tea just too far away for him to hear what the countess is saying.

W. Somerset Maugham 1874–1965
English novelist

🐛 He was imperfect, unfinished, inartistic; he was worse than provincial – he was parochial.

Henry James 1843–1916
American novelist
(of H. D. Thoreau)

🐛 He made a most delible impression on me.

Anonymous

❦ Father's birthday. He would have been ninety-
six, ninety-six, yes, today; and could have
been ninety-six, like other people one has
known: but mercifully was not. His life
would have utterly ended mine.

Virginia Woolf 1882–1941
English novelist

❦ I enjoyed talking to her, but thought nothing
of her writing. I considered her 'a beautiful
little knitter'.

Edith Sitwell 1887–1964
English poet and critic
(of Virginia Woolf)

❦ The scratching of pimples on the body of
the bootboy at Claridges.

Virginia Woolf 1882–1941
English novelist
(of James Joyce's Ulysses)

❦ E. M. Forster never gets any further than warming the teapot. He's a rare fine hand at that. Feel this teapot. Is it not beautifully warm? Yes, but there ain't going to be no tea.

Katherine Mansfield 1888–1923
New Zealand-born short-story writer

❦ A dogged attempt to cover the universe with mud, an inverted Victorianism, an attempt to make crossness and dirt succeed where sweetness and light failed.

E. M. Forster 1879–1970
English novelist
(of James Joyce's *Ulysses*)

❦ And I'll stay off Verlaine too; he was always chasing Rimbauds.

Dorothy Parker 1893–1967
American critic and humorist

❦ Not body enough to cover his mind decently
with; his intellect is improperly exposed.

Sydney Smith 1771–1845
English clergyman and essayist

❦ That poor man. He's completely unspoiled
by failure.

Noël Coward 1899–1973
English playwright, actor and composer

❦ Leavis demands moral earnestness; I prefer
morality . . . I mean I'd sooner live among
people who don't cheat at cards than
among people who are earnest about
not cheating at cards.

C. S. Lewis 1898–1963
Irish-born literary scholar

❦ Scott, the superlative of my comparative.

Lord Byron 1788–1824
English poet

❦ He understood . . . Walt Whitman who laid
end to end words never seen in each other's
company before outside of a dictionary, and
Herman Melville who split the atom of the
traditional novel in the effort to make
whaling a universal metaphor.

David Lodge 1935—
English novelist

❦ The high-water mark, so to speak, of
Socialist literature is W. H. Auden,
a sort of gutless Kipling.

George Orwell 1903–50
English novelist

❦ His sayings are generally like women's letters: all the pith is in the postscript.

William Hazlitt 1778–1830
English essayist

❦ Paul Getty . . . had always been vastly, immeasurably wealthy, and yet went about looking like a man who cannot quite remember whether he remembered to turn the gas off before leaving home.

Bernard Levin 1928—
British journalist

❦ He washed himself with oriental scrupulosity.

Samuel Johnson 1709–84
English poet, critic and lexicographer
(of Jonathan Swift)

❦ The thought of him [William Morris] has always slightly irritated me. Of course he was a wonderfully all-round man, but the act of walking round him has always tired me.

Max Beerbohm 1872–1956
English critic and caricaturist

❦ Gertrude Stein's prose-song [*Three Lives*] is a cold, black suet-pudding . . . Cut it at any point, it is the same thing . . . all fat, without nerve.

Wyndham Lewis 1882–1957
British novelist, painter and critic

❦ The mama of dada.

Clifton Fadiman 1904–99
American critic
(of Gertrude Stein)

❧ Two wise acres and a cow.

Noël Coward 1899–1973
English playwright and composer
(describing the Sitwells)

❧ I have often wished I had time to cultivate
modesty . . . But I am too busy thinking
about myself.

Edith Sitwell 1887–1964
English poet and critic

❧ I cannot and will not cut my conscience
to fit this year's fashions.

Lillian Hellman 1905–84
American playwright

❦ Every word she writes is a lie, including
'and' and 'the'.

Mary McCarthy 1912–89
American novelist
(on Lillian Hellman)

❦ Without you, Heaven would be too dull to bear,
And Hell would not be Hell if you were there.

John Sparrow 1906–92
Warden of All Souls College, Oxford
(epitaph for Maurice Bowra)

❦ *Andiatorocte* is the title of a volume of poems
by the Reverend Clarence Walworth. It is a
word borrowed from the Indians and
should, we think, be returned to
them as soon as possible.

Oscar Wilde 1854–1900
Anglo-Irish playwright and poet

❦ A critic is a man who knows the way but
can't drive the car.

Kenneth Tynan 1927–80
English theatre critic

❦ He will lie even when it is inconvenient: the
sign of the true artist.

Gore Vidal 1925—
American novelist and critic

❦ A young Apollo, golden-haired,
Stands dreaming on the verge of strife,
Magnificently unprepared
For the long littleness of life.

Frances Cornford 1886–1960
English poet
(on Rupert Brooke)

❦ She ran the whole gamut of the emotions
from A to B.

Dorothy Parker 1893–1967
American critic and humorist
(of Katharine Hepburn)

❦ That man's ears make him look like a taxi-cab
with both doors open.

Howard Hughes Jnr 1905–76
American industrialist, aviator and film producer
(of Clark Gable)

❦ He walks top-heavily, like a salmon
standing on its tail.

Kenneth Tynan 1927–80
English theatre critic
(of Charles Laughton)

❦ Will the people in the cheaper seats clap
   your hands? All the rest of you, if
   you'll just rattle your jewellery.

John Lennon 1940–80
English pop singer and songwriter
(at a Royal Variety Performance)

❦ The time was out of joint, and he was only too
   delighted to have been born to set it right.

Lytton Strachey 1880 1932
English biographer
(on Cardinal Manning)

❦ He is an old bore. Even the grave
   yawns for him.

Herbert Beerbohm Tree 1852–1917
English actor-manager
(of Israel Zangwill)

❧ What time he can spare from the adornment
of his person he devotes to the neglect of
his duties.

William Hepworth Thompson 1810–86
English classicist
(of Richard Jebb)

❧ Her journalism, like a diamond, will sparkle
more if it is cut.

Raymond Mortimer 1895–1980
English writer and critic
(on Susan Sontag)

❧ Whenever a friend succeeds, a little
something in me dies.

Gore Vidal 1925—
American novelist and critic

❦ Randolph Churchill went into hospital . . . to
   have a lung removed. It was announced that
   the trouble was not 'malignant' . . . it was
   a typical triumph of modern science to
   find the only part of Randolph that
   was not malignant and remove it.

   Evelyn Waugh 1903–66
   English novelist

❦ Tennessee Williams has a strong streak of
   poetry, but I think he has run into the ground
   rather – what with all those neurotic mothers,
   castrations and things.

   Noël Coward 1899–1973
   English playwright, actor and composer

❧ I always say, keep a diary and someday it'll keep you.

Mae West 1892–1980
American film actress

❧ Forty years ago he was Slightly in *Peter Pan*, and you might say that he has been wholly in *Peter Pan* ever since.

Kenneth Tynan 1927–80
English theatre critic
(of Noël Coward)

❧ Oh, for an hour of Herod!

Anthony Hope 1863–1933
English novelist
(at the first night of J. M. Barrie's *Peter Pan*)

❦   Hush, hush,
    Nobody cares!
    Christopher Robin
    Has
    Fallen
    Down-
    Stairs.

J. B. Morton ('Beachcomber') 1893–1975
British journalist

❦   His strongest tastes were negative. He
    abhorred plastics, Picasso, sunbathing and
    jazz – everything in fact that had
    happened in his own lifetime.

Evelyn Waugh 1903–66
English novelist

❦ They are agreeable enough but if they'd been
   books I shouldn't have read them.

Johann Wolfgang von Goethe 1749–1812
German poet, novelist and playwright
(of fellow guests)

❦ I never forget a face, but in your case I'll
   be glad to make an exception.

Groucho Marx 1895–1977
American film comedian

❦ I have no need of your God-damned sympathy.
   I only wish to be entertained by some of your
   grosser reminiscences.

Alexander Woollcott 1887–1943
American writer

❦ Every other inch a gentleman.

Rebecca West 1892–1983
English novelist and journalist
(of Michael Arlen)

❦ The rich stuffing of her digressions almost
kills the flavour of the bird itself.

John Raymond on Rebecca West

❦ The rat historian.

(*Daily Telegraph* misprint when referring to Sir Anthony Blunt)

❦ She was a tigress surrounded by hamsters.

John Biffen 1930—
British Conservative politician
(of Margaret Thatcher)

266

A triumph of the embalmer's art.

Gore Vidal 1925—
American novelist and critic
(of Ronald Reagan)

I am a Ford, not a Lincoln.

Gerald Ford 1909—
38th President of the USA

Most of my friends seem to be either dead, extremely deaf or living on the wrong side of Kent.

John Gielgud 1904–2002

Waldo is one of those people who would be enormously improved by death.

Saki (Hector Hugh Munro) 1870–1916
Scottish writer

❦   Now is not the time to make enemies.

Voltaire 1694–1778
French writer and philosopher
(advised to renounce the devil on his deathbed)

❦   Dear 338171 – or may I call you 338?

Noël Coward 1899–1973
English playwright, actor and composer
(in a letter to T. E. Lawrence under his assumed identity of
Aircraftsman T. E. Shaw No. 338171)

❦   Sir, I have been commissioned by Michael
Joseph to write an autobiography and I
would be grateful to any of your readers
who could tell me what I was doing
between 1960 and 1974.

Jeffrey Bernard 1932–2001
columnist
(a letter in the *New Statesman*)

❧   Never darken my Dior again!

Beatrice Lillie 1894–1989
British comedienne

❧   Bombazine would have shown a deeper
sense of her loss.

Elizabeth Gaskell 1810–65
English novelist

❧   She's the sort of woman who lives for others –
you can always tell the others by their hunted
expression.

C. S. Lewis 1898–1963
Irish-born literary scholar

❦ She was not quite what you would call refined.
She was not quite what you would call
unrefined. She was the kind of person
that keeps a parrot.

Mark Twain 1835–1910
American writer

❦ Don't get too friendly with her, dear, or
you'll find she'll make a nest in your hair.

Noël Coward 1899–1973
English playwright, actor and composer

❦ Her voice is full of money.

F. Scott Fitzgerald 1896–1940
American novelist

He spoke with a certain what-is-it in his voice, and I could see that, if not actually disgruntled, he was far from being gruntled.

P. G. Wodehouse 1881–1975
English writer

She was not so much a person as an implication of dreary poverty, like an open door in a mean house that lets out the smell of cooking cabbage and the screams of children.

Rebecca West 1892–1983
English novelist and journalist

I sometimes wished he would realise that he was poor instead of being that most nerve-racking of phenomena, a rich man without money.

Peter Ustinov 1921—
Russian-born actor, director and writer

❦ What a good thing Adam had. When he said a good thing he knew nobody had said it before.

Mark Twain 1835–1910
American writer

❦ He would, wouldn't he?

Mandy Rice-Davies 1944—
English courtesan
(at the trial of Stephen Ward, 29 June 1963, on being
told that Lord Astor claimed that her allegations were untrue)

❦ After sitting next to Mr Gladstone I thought he was the cleverest man in England. But after sitting next to Mr Disraeli I thought I was the cleverest woman in England.

Princess Marie Lousie, Queen Victoria's granddaughter

❦ With history one can never be certain, but I
think I can safely say that Artistotle Onassis
would not have married Mrs Khrushchev.

Gore Vidal 1925—
American novelist and critic
(on being asked what would have happened
had Khrushchev and not Kennedy been assassinated)

❦ George III
Ought never to have occurred
One can only wonder
At so grotesque a blunder.

Edmund Clerihew Bentley 1875–1956
English writer

❦ Harris, I am not well; pray get me a glass
of brandy.

King George IV 1762–1830
(on first seeing his future wife, Caroline of Brunswick)

❦ For seventeen years he did nothing at all
but kill animals and stick in stamps.

Sir Harold Nicolson 1886–1968
English diplomat, politician, and writer
(of King George V)

❦ King George, passing slowly in a closed car,
looking like a big, rather worn penny in
the window.

Geoffrey Madan 1895–1947
English bibliophile
(of King George V)

❦ After I am dead, the boy will ruin himself in
twelve months.

King George V 1865–1936
(on his son, the future King Edward VIII)

❦ All this thrown away for *that* . . . I do not
think you have ever realised the shock which
the attitude you took up caused your family
and the whole nation. It seemed inconceivable
to those who had made such sacrifices during
the war that you, as their king, refused a lesser
sacrifice.

Queen Mary 1867–1953
Queen Consort of George V
(letter to the Duke of Windsor on his abdication)

❦ An odious exhibition of journalists dabbling
their fingers in the stuff of other people's souls.

Lord McGregor 1921—
British sociologist
(on press coverage of the marital difficulties of the
Prince and Princess of Wales)

An Appearance
of Solidity

❦ Political language . . . is designed to make lies sound truthful and murder respectable, and to give an appearance of solidity to pure wind.

George Orwell 1903–50
English novelist

❦ Politics is supposed to be the second oldest profession. I have come to realize that it bears a very close resemblance to the first.

Ronald Reagan 1911
40th President of the United States and former Hollywood actor

❦ A sympathiser would seem to imply a certain degree of benevolent feeling. Nothing of the kind. It signifies a ready-made accomplice in any species of political villainy.

Thomas Love Peacock 1785–1866
English novelist and poet

🐦 Men enter local politics solely as a result of being unhappily married.

C. Northcote Parkinson 1909–93
English writer

🐦 What that Sicilian mule was to me, I have been to the Queen.

W. E. Gladstone 1809–98
British Liberal politician

🐦 States, like men, have their growth, their manhood, their decrepitude, their decay.

Walter Savage Landor 1775–1864
English poet

❦ The first duty of a state is to see that every
child born therein shall be well housed,
clothed, fed and educated, till it attain
years of discretion.

John Ruskin 1819–1900
English art and social critic

❦ I do not much like to see a Whig in any dress;
but I hate to see a Whig in a parson's gown.

Samuel Johnson 1709–84
English poet, critic and lexicographer

❦ Damn it! Another bishop dead! I believe they
die to vex me.

William Lamb, 2nd Lord Melbourne 1779–1848
British Whig politician

❧ The illustrious bishop of Cambrai was of more worth than his chambermaid, and there are few of us that would hesitate to pronounce, if his palace were in flames, and the life of only one of them could be preserved, which of the two ought to be preferred.

William Godwin 1756–1836
English philosopher and novelist

❧ Lord Palmerston, with characteristic levity, had once said that only three men in Europe had ever understood [the Schleswig–Holstein question], and of these the Prince Consort was dead, a Danish statesman [unnamed] was in an asylum, and he himself had forgotten it.

Lord Palmerston 1784–1865
British politician

❧ Forever posed between a cliché and an indiscretion.

Harold Macmillan 1894–1986
British Conservative politician
(on the lot of a foreign secretary)

❧ We do not want Egypt any more than any rational man with an estate in the north of England and a residence in the south would have wished to possess the inns on the north road. All he could want would have been that the inns should be well kept, always accessible and furnishing him, when he came, with mutton chops and post horses.

Lord Palmerston 1784–1865
British politician

❦ Our first site in Egypt, be it by larceny or be it by emption, will be the almost certain egg of a North African Empire, that will grow and grow until another Victoria and another Albert, titles of the Lake-sources of the White Nile, come within our borders; and till we finally join hands across the Equator with Natal and Cape Town, to say nothing of the Trasvaal and the Orange River on the south, or of Abyssinia or Zanzibar to be swallowed by way of *viaticum* on our journey.

W.E. Gladstone 1809–98
British Liberal politician

❧ What all the wise men promised has not happened, and what all the damned fools said would happen has come to pass.

William Lamb, 2nd Lord Melbourne 1779–1848
British Whig politician

❧ My mission is to pacify Ireland.

W. E. Gladstone 1809–98
British Liberal politician

❧ I believe they went out, like all good things, with the Stuarts.

Benjamin Disraeli 1804–81
British Conservative politician and novelist

❦ The agonies of a man who has to finish a
difficult negotiation and at the same time to
entertain four royalties at a country house
can be better imagined than described.

Lord Salisbury 1830–1903
British Conservative politician

❦ Assassination is the extreme form of censorship.

George Bernard Shaw 1856–1950
Irish playwright

❦ The only safe pleasure for a parliamentarian
is a bag of boiled sweets.

Julian Critchley 1930–2000
British Conservative politician and journalist

❧ We are bound to lose Ireland in consequence of
years of cruelty, stupidity and misgovernment
and I would rather lose her as a friend than
as a foe.

W. E. Gladstone 1809–98
British Liberal politician

❧ The lamps are going out all over Europe; we
shall not see them lit again in our lifetime.

Sir Edward Grey 1862–1933
British Liberal politician

❧ Negotiating with de Valera . . . is like trying to
pick up mercury with a fork.

David Lloyd George 1863–1945
British Liberal politician
(to which de Valera replied,
'Why doesn't he use a spoon?')

❦ For twenty years he has held a season-ticket on
the line of least resistance and has gone
wherever the train of events has carried him,
lucidly justifying his position at whatever point
he has happened to find himself.

Leo Amery 1873–1955
(on Herbert Asquith)

❦ There is something that governments care far
more for than human life, and that is the
security of property, and so it is through
property that we shall strike the enemy . . .
I say to the government: You have not
dared to take the leaders of Ulster for their
incitement to rebellion. Take me if you dare.

Emmeline Pankhurst 1858–1928
English suffragette leader

❦   I am haunted by mental decay such as I saw
    creeping over Ramsay MacDonald. A
    gradual dimming of the lights.

Sir Harold Nicolson 1886–1968
English diplomat, politician and writer

❦   Let us therefore brace ourselves to our duty,
    and so bear ourselves that, if the British
    Commonwealth and its Empire last for
    a thousand years, men will still say,
    'This was their finest hour.'

Winston Churchill 1874–1965
British Conservative politician

❦ The whole world is in revolt. Soon there will be only five kings left – the King of England, the King of Spades, the King of Clubs, the King of Hearts and the King of Diamonds.

Farouk 1920–65
King of Egypt

❦ We shall not flag or fail. We shall go on to the end. We shall fight in France, we shall fight on the seas and oceans, we shall fight with growing confidence and growing strength in the air, we shall defend our island, whatever the cost may be. We shall fight on the beaches, we shall fight on the landing grounds, we shall fight in the fields and in the streets, we shall fight in the hills; we shall never surrender.

Winston Churchill 1874–1965
British Conservative politician

❧ I have never met anyone who wasn't against
war. Even Hitler and Mussolini were,
according to themselves.

Sir David Low 1891–1963
British political cartoonist

❧ Now this is not the end. It is not even the
beginning of the end. But it is, perhaps,
the end of the beginning.

Winston Churchill 1874–1965
British Conservative politician

❧ War settles nothing . . . to win a war is as
disastrous as to lose one!

Agatha Christie 1890–1976
English writer of detective fiction

❧ I cannot forecast to you the action of Russia.
It is a riddle wrapped in a mystery inside
an enigma.

Winston Churchill 1874–1965
British Conservative politician

❧ Nature has no cure for this sort of madness
[Bolshevism], though I have known a legacy
from a rich relative work wonders.

F. E. Smith 1872–1930
British Conservative politician and lawyer

❧ Business carried on as usual during alterations
on the map of Europe.

Winston Churchill 1874–1965
British Conservative politician

🐦 Ponderous and uncertain is that relation between pressure and resistance which constitutes the balance of power. The arch of peace is morticed by no iron tendons . . . One night a handful of dust will patter from the vaulting: the bats will squeak and wheel in sudden panic: nor can the fragile fingers of man then stay the rush and rumble of destruction.

Harold Nicolson 1886–1968
English diplomat, politician and writer

🐦 We shall have to walk and live a Woolworth life hereafter.

Harold Nicolson 1886–1968
English diplomat, politician and writer
(anticipating the aftermath of the Second World War)

❦ Though I yield to no one in my admiration
for Mr Coolidge, I do wish he did not look
as if he had been weaned on a pickle.

Anonymous

❦ He [Calvin Coolidge] slept more than any other
president, whether by day or by night. Nero
fiddled, but Coolidge only snored.

H. L. Mencken 1880–1956
American journalist and literary critic

❦ Coolidge is a better example of evolution
than either Bryan or Darrow, for he knows
when not to talk, which is the biggest asset
the monkey possesses over the human.

Will Rogers 1879–1935
American actor and humorist

❦ Mr Coolidge's genius for inactivity is developed to a very high point. It is far from being an indolent activity. It is a grim, determined, alert inactivity which keeps Mr Coolidge occupied constantly. Nobody has ever worked harder at inactivity, with such force of character, with such unremitting attention to detail, with such conscientious devotion to the task.

Walter Lippmann 1889–1974
American journalist

❦ How could they tell?

Dorothy Parker 1893–1967
American critic and humorist
(on being told that Calvin Coolidge had died)

❦ A speech from Ernest Bevin on a major
occasion had all the horrific fascination of a
public execution. If the mind was left immune,
eyes and ears and emotions were riveted.

Michael Foot 1913—
British Labour politician

❦ He [Aneurin Bevan] enjoys prophesying the
imminent fall of the capitalist system and is
prepared to play a part, any part, in its burial,
except that of mute.

Harold Macmillan 1894–1986
British Conservative politician

❦ A sheep in sheep's clothing.

Winston Churchill 1874–1965
British Conservative politician
(on Clement Attlee)

❧ I am not, and never have been, a man of the
right. My position was on the left and is
now in the centre of politics.

Oswald Mosley 1896–1980
English Fascist leader

❧ I would remind you that extremism in the
defence of liberty is no vice! And let me
remind you also that moderation in the
pursuit of justice is no virtue!

Barry Goldwater 1909–98
American politician

❧ The Stag at Bay with the mentality of a fox
at large.

Bernard Levin 1928—
British journalist
(of Harold Macmillan)

❦   I thought the best thing to do was to settle up
    these little local difficulties, and then turn to
    the wider vision of the Commonwealth.

> Harold Macmillan 1894–1986
> British Conservative politician
> (following cabinet resignations at home)

❦   The wind of change is blowing through this
    continent, and, whether we like it or not, this
    growth of [African] national consciousness
    is a political fact.

> Harold Macmillan 1894–1986
> British Conservative politician

❦   Greater love hath no man than this, that he
    lay down his friends for his life.

> Jeremy Thorpe 1929—
> British Liberal politician
> (on Harold Macmillan sacking seven of his cabinet)

❦ First of all the Georgian silver goes, and then all that nice furniture that used to be in the saloon. Then the Canalettos go.

Harold Macmillan 1894–1986
British Conservative politician
(on privatisation)

❦ In politics, I think it is wiser to leave five minutes too soon that to continue for five years too long.

John Biffen 1930—
British Conservative politician

❦ I was determined that no British government should be brought down by the action of two tarts.

Harold Macmillan 1894–1986
British Conservative politician
(on the Profumo affair)

Between them, then, Walrus and Carpenter,
they divided up the sixties.

Bernard Levin 1928—
British journalist
(of the Harolds, Macmillan and Wilson)

If he ever went to school without any boots it
was because he was too big for them.

Ivor Bulmer-Thomas 1905–93
British Conservative politician
(on Harold Wilson)

As far as the fourteenth earl is concerned, I
suppose Mr Wilson, when you come to think of
it, is the fourteenth Mr Wilson.

Lord Home 1903–95
British Conservative politician

❦ I think sometimes the prime minister should be intimidating. There's not much point in being a weak, floppy thing in a chair, is there?

Margaret Thatcher 1925—
British Conservative stateswoman

❦ We all know that prime ministers are wedded to the truth, but like other married couples they sometimes live apart.

Saki (Hector Hugh Munro) 1870–1916
Scottish writer

❦ In exceptional circumstances it is necessary to say something that is untrue in the House of Commons.

William Waldegrave 1946—
British Conservative politician

❦ Never contradict.
Never explain.
Never apologise.

John Arbuthnot Fisher 1841–1920
British admiral

❦ I brought myself down. I gave them a sword.
And they stuck it in.

Richard Milhous Nixon 1913–94
37th President of the USA

❦ He immatures with age.

Harold Wilson 1916–95
British Labour politician
(on Tony Benn)

❧ There are three bodies no sensible man directly challenges: the Roman Catholic Church, the Brigade of Guards and the National Union of Mineworkers.

Harold Macmillan 1894–1986
British Conservative politician

❧ Unlike my predecessors, I have devoted more of my life to shunting and hooting than to hunting and shooting.

Sir Fred Burrows 1887–1973
President of the National Union of Railwayman

❧ I hear a smile.

Richard Assheton, Viscount Cross 1823–1914
British Conservative politician
(when the House of Lords laughed
at his speech in favour of Spiritual Peers)

☙ It is not necessary that every time he rises
he should give his famous imitation of a
semi-house-trained polecat.

Michael Foot 1913—
British Labour politician
(of Norman Tebbit)

☙ They've got to draw in their horns and stop
their aggression, or we're going to bomb them
back into the Stone Age.

Curtis E. LeMay 1906–90
US Air-Force officer
(on the North Vietnamese)

❦ We are especially not going to tolerate these attacks from outlaw states run by the strangest collection of misfits, Looney Tunes and squalid criminals since the advent of the Third Reich.

Ronald Reagan 1911—
40th President of the United States and former Hollywood actor

❦ What I want is men who will support me when I am in the wrong.

William Lamb, 2nd Lord Melbourne 1779–1848
British Whig politician

❦ Anyone who isn't confused doesn't really understand the situation.

Ed Murrow 1908–65
American broadcaster and journalist
(on the Vietnam War)

❧ So in your discussions of the nuclear freeze
proposals, I urge you to beware the temptation
of pride – the temptation blithely to declare
yourselves above it all and label both sides
equally at fault, to ignore the facts of history
and the aggressive impulses of an evil empire.

Ronald Reagan 1911—
40th President of the United States and former Hollywood actor

❧ Catholics and Communists have committed
great crimes, but at least they have not stood
aside, like an established society, and been
indifferent. I would rather have blood on my
hands than water like Pilate.

Graham Greene 1904–91
English novelist

❧ I made my mistakes, but in all my years of
public life, I have never profited, never profited
from public service. I've earned every cent. And
in all of my years in public life, I have never
obstructed justice . . . I welcome this kind of
examination because people have got to know
whether or not their president is a crook.
Well, I'm not a crook.

Richard Milhous Nixon 1913–94
37th President of the USA

❧ Being an MP feeds your vanity and starves
your self-respect.

Matthew Parris 1949—
British journalist and former politician

❦ Democrats object to men being disqualified by
   the accident of birth; tradition objects to their
   being disqualified by the accident of death.

G. K. Chesterton 1874–1936
English essayist, novelist and poet

❦ There is no stronger craving in the world than
   that of the rich for titles, except perhaps
   that of the titled for riches.

Hesketh Pearson 1887–1964
English actor and biographer

❦ When I want a peerage, I shall buy it like an
   honest man.

Lord Northcliffe 1865–1922
British newspaper proprietor

❦ Peers: a kind of eye-shade or smoked glass
to protect us from the full glare of Royalty.

Geoffrey Madan 1895–1947
English bibliophile

❦ An aristocracy in a republic is like a chicken
whose head has been cut off: it may run about
in a lively way, but in fact it is dead.

Nancy Mitford 1904–73
English writer

❦ Democracy means government by the
uneducated, while aristocracy means
government by the badly educated.

G. K. Chesterton 1874–1936
English essayist, novelist and poet

❧ I never could believe that Providence had sent a few men into the world, ready booted and spurred, to ride, and millions, ready saddled and bridled, to be ridden.

Richard Rumbold c.1622–85
English republican conspirator

❧ I can't help feeling wary when I hear anything said about the masses. First you take their faces from 'em by calling 'em the masses and then you accuse 'em of not having any faces.

J. B. Priestley 1894–1984
English novelist, playwright and critic

❧ Really, if the lower orders don't set us a good example, what on earth is the use of them?

Oscar Wilde 1854–1900
Anglo-Irish playwright and poet

❧ Most memorable . . . was the discovery (made by all the rich men in England at once) that women and children could work twenty-five hours a day in factories without many of them dying or becoming excessively deformed. This was known as the Industrial Revelation.

W. C. Sellar 1898–1951 and R. J. Yeatman 1898–1968
British writers

❧ Which of us . . . is to do the hard and dirty work for the rest – and for what pay? Who is to do the pleasant and clean work, and for what pay?

John Ruskin 1819–1900
English art and social critic

❦ To the ordinary working man, the sort you
would meet in any pub on Saturday night,
Socialism does not mean much more than
better wages and shorter hours and nobody
bossing you about.

George Orwell 1903–50
English novelist

❦ In a Lancashire cotton-town you could probably
go for months on end without once hearing
an 'educated' accent, whereas there can hardly
be a town in the South of England where you
could throw a brick without hitting the
niece of a bishop.

George Orwell 1903–50
English novelist

❧ Being an MP is the sort of job all working-class parents want for their children – clean, indoors and no heavy lifting.

Diane Abbott 1953—
British Labour politician

❧ You will find as you grow older that the weight of rages will press harder and harder upon the employer.

William Archibald Spooner 1844–1930
English clergyman

❧ The most radical revolutionary will become a conservative on the day after the revolution.

Hannah Arendt 1906–75
American political philosopher

❦ An office party is not, as is sometimes supposed, the managing director's chance to kiss the tea-girl. It is the tea-girl's chance to kiss the managing director . . . Bringing down the mighty from their seats is an agreeable and necessary pastime, but no one supposes that the mighty, having struggled so hard to get seated, will enjoy the dethronement.

Katharine Whitehorn 1926—
English journalist

❦ Conservative ideal of freedom and progress: everyone to have an unfettered opportunity of remaining exactly where they are.

Geoffrey Madan 1895–1947
English bibliophile

❦ Communism in like prohibition, it's a good
   idea but it won't work.

Will Rogers 1879–1935
American actor and humorist

❦ The typical Socialist is . . . a prim little man
   with a white-collar job, usually a secret
   teetotaller and often with vegetarian leanings,
   with a history of Nonconformity behind
   him, and, above all, with a social position
   which he has no intention of forfeiting.

George Orwell 1903–50
English novelist

❦ Let us be frank about it: most of our people
   have never had it so good.

Harold Macmillan 1894–1986
British Conservative politician

❧ The British bourgeoisie
Is not born,
And does not die,
But, if it is ill,
It has a frightened look in its eyes.

Osbert Sitwell 1892–1969
English writer

❧ Destroy him as you will, the bourgeois always
bounces up – execute him, expropriate him,
starve him out *en masse*, and he reappears
in your children.

Cyril Connolly 1903–74
English writer

❧ A person of bourgeois origin goes through life with some expectation of getting what he wants, within reasonable limits. Hence the fact that in times of stress 'educated' people tend to come to the front.

George Orwell 1903–50
English novelist

❧ We of the sinking middle class . . . may sink without further struggles into the working class where we belong, and probably when we get there it will not be so dreadful as we feared, for, after all, we have nothing to lose but our aitches.

George Orwell 1903–50
English novelist

❧ Laws are generally found to be nets of such a
texture as the little creep through, the great
break through and the middle-sized are
alone entangled in.

William Shenstone 1714–63
English poet and essayist

❧ As I look ahead, I am filled with foreboding.
Like the Roman, I seem to see 'the River Tiber
foaming with much blood'.

Enoch Powell 1912–98
British Conservative politician
(on unrestricted immigration)

❧ The function of a government is to calm
rather than to excite agitation.

Lord Palmerston 1784–1865
British politician

❧ Call a thing immoral or ugly, soul-destroying or a degradation of man, a peril to the peace of the world or to the well-being of future generations: as long as you have not shown it to be 'uneconomic' you have not really questioned its right to exist, grow and prosper.

E. F. Schumacher 1911–77
German-born economist

❧ Trickle-down theory – the less than elegant metaphor that if one feeds the horse enough oats, some will pass through to the road for the sparrows.

J. K. Galbraith 1908—
Canadian-born American economist

🍇 Our whole economy is based on planned
obsolescence . . . we make good products,
we induce people to buy them, and then the
next year we deliberately introduce something
that will make these products old-fashioned,
out of date, obsolete.

Brooks Stevens
American industrial designer

🍇 A government which robs Peter to pay Paul can
always depend on the support of Paul.

George Bernard Shaw 1856–1950
Irish playwright

🍇 To betray, you must first belong.

Kim Philby 1912–88
British intelligence officer and Soviet spy

❦ Management that wants to change an
institution must first show it loves
that institution.

John Tusa 1936—
British broadcaster and radio journalist

❦ I didn't fight to get women out from behind
the vacuum cleaner to get them on to the
board of Hoover.

Germaine Greer 1939—
Australian feminist

❦ A diplomat these days is nothing but a head-
waiter who's allowed to sit down occasionally.

Peter Ustinov 1921—
Russian-born actor, director and writer

❦ The gallery in which the reporters sit has
   become a fourth estate of the realm.

   Thomas Babington, 1st Baron Macaulay 1800–59
   English politician and historian

❦ I'm with you on the free press. It's the
   newspapers I can't stand.

   Tom Stoppard 1937—
   British playwright

❦ Never lose your temper with the press or the
   public is a major rule of political life.

   Christabel Pankhurst 1880–1958
   English suffragette

❦ This is a free country, madam. We have a right to share your privacy in a public place.

Peter Ustinov 1921—
Russian-born actor, director and writer

❦ Corruption, the most infallible symptom of constitutional liberty.

Edward Gibbon 1737–94
English historian

❦ The South African police would leave no stone unturned to see that nothing disturbed the even terror of their lives.

Tom Sharpe 1928—
English writer

'Yes, but not in the South.'

❦ 'Yes, but not in the South', with slight
adjustments, will do for any argument about
any place, if not about any person.

Stephen Potter 1900–69
British writer

❦ Mr Huxley assures me that it's no farther from
the north coast of Spitzbergen to the North
Pole than it is from Land's End to
John of Gaunt.

William Archibald Spooner 1844–1930
English clergyman

❦ Nationalism is an infantile sickness. It is
the measles of the human race.

Albert Einstein 1879–1955
German-born theoretical physicist

❧ England . . . resembles a family, a rather stuffy Victorian family, with not many black sheep in it but with all its cupboards bursting with skeletons. It has rich relations who have to be kowtowed to and poor relations who are horribly sat upon, and there is a deep conspiracy of silence about the source of the family income. It is a family in which the young are generally thwarted and most of the power is in the hands of irresponsible uncles and bed-ridden aunts. Still, it is a family. It has its private language and its common memories, and at the approach of an enemy it closes its ranks. A family with the wrong members in control.

George Orwell 1903–50
English novelist

❦ English policy is to float lazily downstream,
occasionally putting out a diplomatic
boat-hook to avoid collision.

Lord Salisbury 1830–1903
British Conservative politician

❦ Down here it was still the England I had known
in my childhood: the railway cuttings
smothered in wild flowers . . . the red buses, the
blue policemen – all sleeping the deep, deep
sleep of England, from which I sometimes fear
that we shall never wake till we are jerked out of
it by the roar of bombs.

George Orwell 1903–50
English novelist

❧ Love of our country is another of those
   specious illusions which have been
   invented by impostors in order to render
   the multitude the blind instruments of their
   crooked designs.

William Godwin 1756–1836
English philosopher and novelist

❧ Ask any man what nationality he would
   prefer to be, and ninety-nine out of a
   hundred will tell you that they would
   prefer to be Englishmen.

Cecil Rhodes 1853–1902
South African statesman

❧ Norway, too, has noble wild prospects; and Lapland is remarkable for prodigious noble wild prospects. But, sir, let me tell you, the noblest prospect which a Scotchman ever sees is the high road that leads him to England!

Samuel Johnson 1709–84
English poet, critic and lexicographer

❧ Frogs . . . are slightly better than Huns or Wops, but abroad is unutterably bloody and foreigners are fiends.

Nancy Mitford 1904–73
English writer

- The notion of liberty amuses the people of England and helps to keep off the *taedium vitae*. When a butcher tells you that his heart bleeds for his country he has, in fact, no uneasy feeling.

Samuel Johnson 1709–84
English poet, critic and lexicographer

- If an earthquake were to engulf England tomorrow, the English would manage to meet and dine somewhere among the rubbish, just to celebrate the event.

Douglas Jerrold 1803–57
English playwright and journalist

❦ An Englishman, even if he is alone, forms an orderly queue of one.

George Mikes 1912–87
Hungarian-born writer

❦ In England, justice is open to all – like the Ritz Hotel.

Sir James Mathew 1830–1908
Irish judge

❦ We know no spectacle so ridiculous as the British public in one of its periodical fits of morality.

Thomas Babington, 1st Baron Macaulay 1800–59
English politician and historian

❦ Most English talk is a quadrille in a sentry-box.

Henry James 1843–1916
American novelist

❦ The English have no respect for their language, and will not teach their children to speak it. They spell it so abominably that no man can teach himself what it sounds like. It is impossible for an Englishman to open his mouth without making some other Englishman hate or despise him.

George Bernard Shaw 1856–1950
Irish playwright

❦ You will hear more good things on the outside of a stagecoach from London to Oxford than if you were to pass a twelvemonth with the undergraduates, or heads of colleges, of that famous university.

William Hazlitt 1778–1830
English essayist

❦ City of perspiring dreams.

Frederic Raphael 1931—
British novelist and screenwriter
(of Cambridge)

❦ To the University of Oxford I acknowledge no
obligation; and she will as cheerfully renounce
me for a son, as I am willing to disclaim her for
a mother. I spent fourteen months at Magdalen
College: they proved the fourteen months the
most idle and unprofitable of my whole life.

Edward Gibbon 1737–94
English historian

❦ The Vicar of St Ives says the smell of fish
there is sometimes so terrific as to stop
the church clock.

Francis Kilvert 1840–79
English clergyman and diarist

❦ I think the British have the distinction above all other nations of being able to put new wine into old bottles without bursting them.

Clement Attlee 1883–1967
British Labour politician

❦ Britain will be honoured by historians more for the way she disposed of an empire than for the way in which she acquired it.

Lord Harlech 1918–85
British Ambassador to Washington

❦ The best thing I know between France and England is – the sea.

Douglas Jerrold 1803–57
English playwright and journalist

❦ You must consider every man your enemy who speaks ill of your king; and . . . you must hate a Frenchman as you hate the devil.

Horatio, Lord Nelson 1758–1805
British admiral

❦ There is nothing so bad or so good that you will not find Englishmen doing it; but you will never find an Englishman in the wrong. He does everything on principle. He fights you on patriotic principles; he robs you on business principles; he enslaves you on imperial principles; he bullies you on manly principles; he supports his king on loyal principles and cuts off his king's head on republican principles.

George Bernard Shaw 1856–1950
Irish playwright

❦ I have heard some say . . . [homosexual]
  practices are allowed in France and in other
  NATO countries. We are not French, and
  we are not other nationals. We are
  British, thank God!

Viscount Montgomery of Alamein 1887–1976
British field marshal

❦ Do you know what 'le vice Anglais' – the
  English vice – really is? Not flagellation, not
  pederasty – whatever the French believe it to
  be. It's our refusal to admit our emotions. We
  think they demean us, I suppose.

Terence Rattigan 1911–77
English playwright

❧ It is not that the Englishman can't feel – it is that he is afraid to feel. He has been taught at his public school that feeling is bad form. He must not express great joy or sorrow. Or even open his mouth too wide when he talks – his pipe might fall out if he did.

E. M. Forster 1879–1970
English novelist

❧ What a pity it is that we have no amusements in England but vice and religion!

Sydney Smith 1771–1845
English clergyman and essayist

❧ The flushpots of Euston and the hanging garments of Marylebone.

James Joyce 1882–1941
Irish novelist

❧ An acre in Middlesex is better than a principality in Utopia.

Thomas Babington, 1st Baron Macaulay 1800–59
English politician and historian

❧ Byron said that the only way of conquering cant (and hypocrisy) was ridicule – 'the only weapon that the English climate cannot rust'.

Lord Byron 1788–1824
English poet

❧ The way to ensure summer in England is to have it framed and glazed in a comfortable room.

Horace Walpole 1717–97
English writer and connoisseur

❦ Righteous indignation . . . is misplaced if we
agree with the lady's maid that high birth is a
form of congenital insanity, that the sufferer
merely inherits diseases of his ancestors, and
endures them, for the most part very stoically,
in one of those comfortably padded lunatic
asylums which are known, euphemistically, as
the stately homes of England.

Virginia Woolf 1882–1941
English novelist

❦ I could come back to America . . . to die – but
never, never to live.

Henry James 1843–1916
American novelist

❦ There are no second acts in American lives.

F. Scott Fitzgerald 1896–1940
American novelist

❦ In the United States there is more space where nobody is than where anybody is. That is what makes America what it is.

Gertrude Stein 1874–1946
American writer

❦ A big hard-boiled city with no more personality than a paper cup.

Raymond Chandler 1888–1959
American writer of detective fiction
(of Los Angeles)

❦ 'There won't be any revolution in America,' said
Isadore. Nikitin agreed. 'The people are all too
clean. They spend all their time changing their
shirts and washing themselves. You can't feel
fierce and revolutionary in a bathroom.'

Eric Linklater 1899–1974
Scottish novelist

❦ 'Do you pray for the senators, Dr Hale?'
'No, I look at the senators and I pray for the
country.'

Edward Everett Hale 1822–1909
American clergyman

❦ America, thou half-brother of the world;
With something good and bad of every land.

Philip James Bailey 1816–1902
English poet

❧ Poor Mexico, so far from God and so close to the United States.

Porfirio Diaz 1830–1915
President of Mexico

❧ Doctor, my doctor, what do you say, let's put the id back in yid!

Philip Roth 1933—
American novelist

❧ In fact, I'm not really a *Jew*. Just Jew-*ish*. Not the whole hog, you know.

Jonathan Miller 1934—
English writer and director

❦ A Jewish man with parents alive is a fifteen-year-old boy, and will remain a fifteen-year-old boy until they die!

Philip Roth 1933—
American novelist

❦ How odd
Of God
To choose
The Jews.

William Norman Ewer 1885–1976
British writer

❦ But not so odd
As those who choose
A Jewish God
But spurn the Jews.

Cecil Browne 1932—
American businessman

❦ Switzerland is a small, steep country, much more up and down than sideways, and is all stuck over with large brown hotels built in the cuckoo-clock style of architecture.

Ernest Hemingway 1899–1961
American novelist

❦ Standing among savage scenery, the hotel offers stupendous revelations. There is a French widow in every bedroom, affording delightful prospects.

Gerard Hoffnung 1925–59
English humorist

❦ In Italy for thirty years under the Borgias they
  had warfare, terror, murder, bloodshed – they
  produced Michelangelo, Leonardo da Vinci
  and the Renaissance. In Switzerland they had
  brotherly love, five hundred years of democracy
  and peace and what did that produce . . . ?
  The cuckoo clock.

Orson Welles 1915–85
American actor and film director
(from *The Third Man*)

❦ STREETS FLOODED. PLEASE ADVISE.

Robert Benchley 1889–1945
American humorist
(telegraph message on arriving in Venice)

❦ It was at Rome, on the fifteenth of October 1764, as I sat musing amidst the ruins of the Capitol, while the barefoot friars were singing vespers in the Temple of Jupiter, that the idea of writing the decline and fall of the city first started to my mind.

Edward Gibbon 1737–94
English historian

❦ The people of Crete unfortunately make more history than they can consume locally.

Saki (Hector Hugh Munro) 1870–1916
Scottish writer

❦ Earth is here so kind, that just tickle her with a hoe and she laughs with a harvest.

Douglas Jerrold 1803–57
English playwright and journalist
(of Australia)

❦ Rule 1, on page 1 of the book of war, is: 'Do not march on Moscow' . . . [Rule 2] is: 'Do not go fighting with your land armies in China.'

Viscount Montgomery of Alamein 1887–1976
British field marshal

❦ Match me such marvel, save in Eastern clime,
A rose-red city – half as old as time!

John William Burgon 1813–88
English clergyman

❦ 'Back to Glasgow to do some work for the cause,' I said lightly.
'Just so,' he said, with a grin. 'It's a great life if you don't weaken.'

John Buchan 1875–1940
Scottish novelist

❦ I come from suburbia . . . and I don't ever want
to go back. It's the one place in the world
that's farther away than anywhere else.

Frederic Raphael 1931—
British novelist and screenwriter

❦ Pleasure resorts are like film stars and
royalty . . . embarrassed by the figures they
cut in the fantasies of people who have never
met them.

Doris Lessing 1919—
English writer

❦ A man travels the world in search of what he
needs and returns home to find it.

George Moore 1852–1933
Anglo-Irish novelist

That Vast
Moth-Eaten
Musical Brocade

❦ Religion . . .
That vast moth-eaten musical brocade,
Created to pretend we never die.

Philip Larkin 1922–85
English poet

❦ Religion's in the heart, not in the knees.

Douglas Jerrold 1803–57
English playwright and journalist

❦ There is only one religion, though there
are a hundred versions of it.

George Bernard Shaw 1856–1950
Irish playwright

❧ To those who believe in God, no explanation is necessary. To those who do not, no explanation is possible.

Anonymous

❧ We're all of us guinea pigs in the laboratory of God. Humanity is just a work in progress.

Tennessee Williams 1911–83
American playwright

❧ The world is not a 'prison house', but a kind of kindergarten, where millions of bewildered infants are trying to spell God with the wrong blocks.

Leo Robin 1900–84
American songwriter

❧ The baby doesn't understand English and
the Devil knows Latin.

Ronald Knox 1888–1957
English writer and Roman Catholic priest
(on being asked to perform a baptism in English)

❧ The Christian ideal has not been tried and
found wanting. It has been found difficult;
and left untried.

G. K. Chesterton 1874–1936
English essayist, novelist and poet

❧ Ten thousand difficulties do not make
one doubt.

John Henry Newman 1801–90
English theologian

❦ I am not clear that God manoeuvres physical
things . . . After all, a conjuring trick with
bones only proves that it is as clever as a
conjuring trick with bones . . . A resuscitated
corpse might be a resuscitated corpse and
might be the sign of something, but there is
still the question of what it is the symbol of.

David Jenkins 1925—
English theologian and Bishop of Durham

❦ We *know* our will is free, and there's an end
on't.

Samuel Johnson 1709–84
English poet, critic and lexicographer

❦ It is the final proof of God's omnipotence that he need not exist in order to save us.

Peter De Vries 1910–93
American novelist

❦ Religion to me has always been the wound, not the bandage.

Dennis Potter 1935–94
English television dramatist

❦ Religions are kept alive by heresies, which are really sudden explosions of faith. Dead religions do not produce them.

Gerald Brenan 1894–1987
British travel writer and novelist

❦ How can what an Englishman believes be heresy? It is a contradiction in terms.

George Bernard Shaw 1856–1950
Irish playwright

❦ Here you could love human beings nearly as God loved them, knowing the worst; you didn't love a pose, a pretty dress, a sentiment artfully assumed.

Graham Greene 1904–91
English novelist

❦ 'I know of no joy,' she airily began, 'greater than a cool white dress after the sweetness of confession.'

Ronald Firbank 1886–1926
English novelist

❧ It's a curious fact that the all-male religions
have produced no religious imagery – in most
cases have positively forbidden it. The great
religious art of the world is deeply involved with
the female principle.

Kenneth Clark 1903–83
English art historian

❧ To give a sex to mind was not very consistent
with the principles of a man [Rousseau] who
argued so warmly, and so well, for the
immortality of the soul.

Mary Wollstonecraft 1759–97
English feminist

❦ A woman's preaching is like a dog's walking
on his hinder legs. It is not done well; but
you are surprised to find it done at all.

Samuel Johnson 1709–84
English poet, critic and lexicographer

❦ Her conception of God was certainly not
orthodox. She felt towards him as she might
have felt towards a glorified sanitary engineer;
and in some of her speculations she seems
hardly to distinguish between the deity
and the drains.

Lytton Stratchey 1880–1932
English biographer
(of Florence Nightingale)

❦ I see it as an elderly lady, who mutters away to
   herself in a corner, ignored most of the time.

George Carey 1935—
Archbishop of Canterbury
(on the Church of England)

❦ An atheist is a man who has no invisible means
   of support.

John Buchan 1875–1940
Scottish novelist

❦ There are no atheists in the foxholes.

William Thomas Cummings 1903–45
American priest

❦ He was an embittered atheist (the sort of atheist
   who does not so much disbelieve in God as
   personally dislike him), and took a sort of
   pleasure in thinking that human affairs would
   never improve.

George Orwell 1903–50
English novelist

❦ Cricket – a game which the English, not being a
   spiritual people, have invented in order to give
   themselves some conception of eternity.

Lord Mancroft 1914–87
British Conservative politician

❦ Eternity's a terrible thought. I mean, where's
   it all going to end?

Tom Stoppard 1937—
British playwright

❧ A decision of the courts ruled that the game
of golf may be played on Sunday, not being a
game within the view of the law, but being
a form of moral effort.

Stephen Leacock 1869–1944
Canadian humorist

❧ You can tell what God thinks of money when
you look at those to whom he has given it.

Anonymous

❧ Prove to me that you're no fool.
Walk across my swimming pool.

Tim Rice 1944—
English songwriter

❦ Whatever a man prays for, he prays for a
miracle. Every prayer reduces to this: 'Great
God, grant that twice two be not four.'

Ivan Turgenev 1818–83
Russian novelist

❦ I am just going to pray for you at St Paul's, but
with no very lively hope of success.

Sydney Smith 1771–1845
English clergyman and essayist

❦ God is love, but get it in writing.

Gypsy Rose Lee 1914–70
American striptease artiste

❦ God seems to have left the receiver off the
hook, and time is running out.

Arthur Koestler 1905–83
Hungarian-born writer

❦ If only God would give me some clear sign!
   Like making a large deposit in my name at
   a Swiss bank.

Woody Allen 1935—
American film director, writer and actor

❦ If you talk to God, you are praying; if God talks
   to you, you have schizophrenia. If the dead talk
   to you, you are a spiritualist; if God talks to
   you, you are a schizophrenic.

Thomas Szasz 1920—
Hungarian-born psychiatrist

❦ When suave politeness, tempering bigot zeal,
   Corrected *I believe* to *One does feel*.

Ronald Knox 1888–1957
English writer and Roman Catholic priest

❦ Things have come to a pretty pass when
   religion is allowed to invade the sphere
   of private life.

William Lamb, 2nd Lord Melbourne 1779–1848
British Whig politician

❦ JOHN MORTIMER: You said you were going to
   lie low like Brer Rabbit.
   BISHOP OF DURHAM: That was misinterpreted.
   I only meant that I was going away for the
   weekend.

David Jenkins 1925—
English theologian and Bishop of Durham

❦ If it turns out that there is a God, I don't think that he's evil. But the worst that you can say about him is that basically he's an underachiever.

Woody Allen 1935—
American film director, writer and actor

❦ Everything suffers by translation except a bishop.

Lord Chesterfield 1694–1774
English writer and politician

❦ It was the afternoon of my eighty-first birthday and I was in bed with my catamite when Ali announced that the archbishop had come to see me.

Anthony Burgess 1917–93
English novelist and critic

❦ Them bastards at the monastery let me
down again.

Harold Pinter 1930—
English playwright
(from *The Caretaker*)

❦ Evangelical vicar, in want
Of a portable, second-hand font,
    Would dispose, for the same,
    Of a portrait, in frame,
Of the Bishop, elect, of Vermont.

Ronald Knox 1888–1957
English writer and Roman Catholic priest

❦ It was a blonde. A blonde to make a bishop kick
a hole in a stained-glass window.

Raymond Chandler 1888–1959
American writer of detective fiction

❦ Only on the firm foundation of unyielding
   despair, can the soul's habitation
   henceforth be safely built.

Bertrand Russell 1872–1970
British philosopher and mathematician

❦ Operationally, God is beginning to resemble
   not a ruler but the last fading smile of a
   cosmic Cheshire cat.

Sir Julian Huxley 1887–1975
English biologist

❦ If we find the answer to that [why it is that we
   and the universe exist], it would be the
   ultimate triumph of human reason –
   for then we would know the mind of God.

Stephen Hawking 1942—
English theoretical physicist

❧ My idea of heaven is eating pâté de foie gras
to the sound of trumpets.

Sydney Smith 1771–1845
English clergyman and essayist

We are as near to heaven by sea as by land!

Sir Humphrey Gilbert c. 1537–83
English explorer

❧ Winston Churchill was once referred to as
a pillar of the Church. 'No, no,' he replied,
'not a pillar of the Church but a buttress,
supporting it from the outside.'

Winston Churchill 1875–1965
British Conservative politician

❦ God is really only another artist. He invented the giraffe, the elephant and the cat. He has no real style. He just goes on trying other things.

Pablo Picasso 1881–1973
Spanish painter

One Crowded Hour
of Glorious Life

❧ Sound, sound the clarion, fill the fife,
Throughout the sensual world proclaim,
One crowded hour of glorious life
Is worth an age without a name.

Thomas Osbert Mordaunt 1730–1809
English soldier and poet

❧ Peeling off the kilometres to the tune of 'Blue
Skies', sizzling down the long black liquid
reaches of Nationale Sept, the plane trees
going sha-sha-sha through the open window,
the windscreen yellowing with crushed
midges, she with the *Michelin* beside me,
a handkerchief binding her hair.

Cyril Connolly 1903–74
English writer

❦ Summer afternoon – summer afternoon . . .
the two most beautiful words in the
English language.

Henry James 1843–1916
American novelist

❦ Well, we knocked the bastard off!

Sir Edmund Hillary 1919—
New Zealand mountaineer
(on conquering Mount Everest)

❦ Don't you find it a beautiful clean thought,
a world empty of people, just uninterrupted
grass, and a hare sitting up?

D. H. Lawrence 1885–1930
English novelist and poet

❦ Lost, yesterday, somewhere between sunrise
and sunset, two golden hours, each set with
sixty diamond minutes. No reward is offered,
for they are gone for ever.

Horace Mann 1796–1859
American educationist

❦ It was about eleven o'clock in the morning, mid
October, with the sun not shining and a look of
hard wet rain in the clearness of the foothills. I
was wearing my powder-blue suit, with dark-
blue shirt, tie and display handkerchief, black
brogues, black wool socks with dark blue
clocks on them. I was neat, clean, shaved
and sober, and I didn't care who knew it.

Raymond Chandler 1888–1959
American writer of detective fiction

❦ Live all you can; it's a mistake not to. It doesn't so much matter what you do in particular, so long as you have your life. If you haven't had that, what *have* you had?

Henry James 1843–1916
American novelist

❦ Life is like a very short visit to a toyshop between birth and death.

Desmond Morris 1928—
English anthropologist

❦ In his blue gardens, men and girls came and went like moths among the whisperings and the champagne and the stars.

F. Scott Fitzgerald 1896–1940
American novelist
(from *The Great Gatsby*)

❧ Sir, I look upon every day to be lost in which
I do not make a new acquaintance.

Samuel Johnson 1709–84
English poet, critic and lexicographer

❧ Every man, wherever he goes, is encompassed
by a cloud of comforting convictions, which
move with him like flies on a summer day.

Bertrand Russell 1872–1970
British philosopher and mathematician

❧ So then Dr Froyd said that all I needed was to
cultivate a few inhibitions and get some sleep.

Anita Loos 1893–1981
American writer

❦ Brevity is the soul of lingerie, as the petticoat said to the chemise.

Dorothy Parker 1893–1967
American critic and humorist

❦ An orgy looks particularly alluring seen through the mists of righteous indignation.

Malcolm Muggeridge 1903–90
British journalist

❦ Cheerfulness gives elasticity to the spirit. Spectres fly before it.

Samuel Smiles 1812–1904
English writer

❦ We know little about the conscience except that it is soluble in alcohol.

Anonymous

❦ All men who have turned out worth anything have had the chief hand in their own education.

Sir Walter Scott 1771–1832
Scottish novelist and poet

❦ Not many sounds in life, and I include all urban and all rural sounds, exceed in interest a knock at the door.

Charles Lamb 1775–1834
English writer

❦ It is better to wear out than to rust out.

Richard Cumberland 1631–1718
English divine

❦ [The Pyramids] seem to have been erected only
in compliance with that hunger of imagination
which preys incessantly upon life, and must be
always appeased by some employment . . . I
consider this mighty structure as a monument
to the insufficiency of human enjoyments.

Samuel Johnson 1709–84
English poet, critic and lexicographer

The Most Fatal
Complaint of All

❧ Nothing really wrong with him – only *anno domini*, but that's the most fatal complaint of all, in the end.

James Hilton 1900–54
English novelist

❧ His soul swooned slowly as he heard the snow falling faintly through the universe and faintly falling, like the descent of their last end, upon all the living and the dead.

James Joyce 1882–1941
Irish novelist

❧ It's a funny old world – a man's lucky if he gets out of it alive.

Walter de Leon and Paul M. Jones
(from the film *You're Telling Me*)

❦ When all is done, human life is, at the greatest
and the best, but like a froward child that
must be played with and humoured a little
to keep it quiet till it falls asleep, and then
the care is over.

Sir William Temple 1628–99
English diplomat and essayist

❦ I never think of the future. It comes soon enough.

Albert Einstein 1879–1955
German-born theoretical physicist

❦ We have trained them [men] to think of the
future as a promised land which favoured
heroes attain – not as something which
everyone reaches at the rate of sixty minutes an
hour, whatever he does, whoever he is.

C. S. Lewis 1898–1963
Irish-born literary scholar

❦ I remember my youth and the feeling that will
never come back any more – the feeling that I
could last for ever, outlast the sea, the earth,
and all men; the deceitful feeling that lures us
on to joys, to perils, to love, to vain effort – to
death; the triumphant conviction of strength,
the heat of life in the handful of dust, the glow
in the heart that with every year grows dim,
grows cold, grows small and expires – and
expires, too soon, too soon – before life itself

Joseph Conrad 1857–1924
Polish-born English novelist

❦ Time goes, you say? Ah no!
Alas, time stays, we go.

Henry Austin Dobson 1840–1921
English poet, biographer and essayist

❦ The past is a foreign country; they do things differently there.

L. P. Hartley 1895–1972
English novelist

❦ In a dream, you are never eighty.

Anne Sexton 1928–74
American poet

❦ Ships that pass in the night, and speak to each
    other in passing;
Only a signal shown and a distant voice in the
    darkness;
So on the ocean of life we pass and speak to
    one another;
Only a look and a voice, then darkness again
    and silence.

Henry Wadsworth Longfellow 1807–82
American poet

❧ Whenever I prepare for a journey I prepare as though for death. Should I never return, all is in order.

Katherine Mansfield 1888–1923
New Zealand-born short-story writer

❧ I don't want to achieve immortality through my work . . . I want to achieve it through not dying.

Woody Allen 1935—
American film director, writer and actor

❧ The four stages of man are infancy, childhood, adolescence and obsolescence.

Art Linkletter 1912—
American broadcaster and humorist

❦   A beginning, a muddle, and an end.

Philip Larkin 1922–85
English poet

❦   We are all serving a life-sentence in the
    dungeon of self.

Cyril Connolly 1903–74
English writer

❦   What has one to do, when one grows tired of
    the world . . . but to draw nearer and nearer
    and gently waste the remains of life with friends
    with whom one began it?

Horace Walpole 1717–97
English writer and connoisseur

🌑 So little done, so much to do.

Cecil Rhodes 1853–1902
South African statesman
(said on the day of his death)

🌑 The cares that infest the day
Shall fold their tents, like the Arabs,
And as silently steal away.

Henry Wadsworth Longfellow 1807–82
American poet

🌑 Let us not take too much delight in pleasures
we cannot long enjoy, nor grieve with too much
dejection for evils which cannot long be felt.

Samuel Johnson 1709–84
English poet, critic and lexicographer

❦ Things have dropped from me. I have outlived
  certain desires; I have lost friends, some by
  death – Percival – others through sheer
  inability to cross the street.

Virginia Woolf 1882–1941
English novelist

❦ Growing old is like being increasingly
  penalised for a crime you haven't committed.

Anthony Powell 1905–2000
English novelist

❦ Here I sit, alone and sixty,
  Bald, and fat, and full of sin,
  Cold the seat and loud the cistern,
  As I read the Harpic tin.

Alan Bennett 1934—
English actor and playwright

❧ Take away that emblem of mortality.

Benjamin Disraeli 1804–81
British Conservative politician and novelist
(on being offered an air cushion to sit on)

❧ The abbreviation of time, and the failure of
hope, will always tinge with a browner
shade the evening of life.

Edward Gibbon 1737–94
English historian

❧ Life is too short to stuff a mushroom.

Shirley Conran 1932—
English writer

❧ For there is good news yet to hear and fine
things to be seen,
Before we go to Paradise by way of Kensal
Green.

G. K. Chesterton 1874–1936
English essayist, novelist and poet

❧ There is a wicked inclination in most people to
suppose an old man decayed in his intellects.
If a young or middle-aged man, when leaving a
company, does not recollect where he laid his
hat, it is nothing; but if the same inattention is
discovered in an old man, people will shrug
up their shoulders, and say, 'His memory
is going.'

Samuel Johnson 1709–84
English poet, critic and lexicographer

❧ Women never have young minds. They are born three thousand years old.

Shelagh Delaney 1939—
English playwright

❧ When a man fell into his anecdotage it was a sign for him to retire from the world.

Benjamin Disraeli 1804–81
British Conservative politician and novelist

❧ Babylon in all its desolation is a sight not so awful as that of the human mind in ruins.

Scrope Davies c.1783–1852
English conversationalist

❧ Below my window . . . The blossom is out in
full now . . . I see it is the whitest, frothiest,
blossomiest blossom that there ever could be,
and I can see it. Things are both more trivial
than they ever were, and more important than
they ever were, and the difference between
the trivial and the important doesn't seem
to matter. But the nowness of everything
is absolutely wondrous.

Dennis Potter 1935–94
English television dramatist
(on his heightened awareness of things
in the face of his imminent death)

❧ I now begin the journey that will lead me into
the sunset of my life.

Ronald Reagan 1911—
40th President of the United States and former Hollywood actor
(on the onset of Alzheimer's disease)

❦   So here it is at last, the distinguished thing!

Henry James 1843–1916
American novelist
(on experiencing his first stroke)

We Must All Go to Bed in Another World

One doth but breakfast here, another
dines, he that liveth longest doth but sup;
we must all go to bed in another world.

Joseph Henshaw 1603–79
English divine

. . . Despite all prayers
And curses, health food, face-lifts, drugs,
Something surer than the Bomb
Will close your books, and roll your rugs,
And tip your life into the tomb.

Paul Groves

It's not that I'm afraid to die. I just don't want
to be there when it happens.

Woody Allen 1935—
American film director, writer and actor

❧ Death has got something to be said for it:
There's no need to get out of bed for it;
Wherever you may be,
They bring it to you, free.

Kingsley Amis 1922–95
English novelist and poet

❧ The cradle rocks above an abyss, and common
sense tells us that our existence is but a brief
crack of light between two eternities of
darkness.

Vladimir Nabokov 1899–1977
Russian novelist

❧ In chains and darkness, wherefore should I stay,
And mourn in prison, while I keep the key?

Lady Mary Wortley Montagu 1689–1762
English writer

❦   Let me die a youngman's death,
    Not a clean & in-between-
    The-sheets, holy-water death,
    Not a famous-last-words
    Peaceful out-of-breath death.

Roger McGough 1937—
English poet

❦   If there wasn't death, I think you couldn't go on.

Stevie Smith 1902–71
English poet and novelist

❦   Death has a thousand doors to let out life:
    I shall find one.

Philip Massinger 1583–1640
English playwright

❦ Death opens unknown doors. It is most
grand to die.

John Masefield 1878–1967
English poet

❦ Life is a great surprise. I do not see why death
should not be an even greater one.

Vladimir Nabokov 1899–1977
Russian novelist

❦ Death is nothing at all; it does not count. I
have only slipped away into the next room.

Henry Scott Holland 1847–1918
English theologian and preacher

❦ Death is not anything . . . death is not . . . It's
the absence of presence, nothing more . . . the
endless time of never coming back . . . a gap
you can't see, and when the wind blows
through it, it makes no sound.

Tom Stoppard 1937—
British playwright

❦ The dead don't die. They look on and help.

D. H. Lawrence 1885–1930
English novelist and poet

❦ Fourteen heart attacks and he had to die in my
week. In my week!

Janis Joplin 1943–70
American singer
(when ex-President Eisenhower's death prevented
her photograph appearing on the cover of Newsweek)

❧ Her late husband, you know, a very sad
death – eaten by missionaries – poor soul!

William Archibald Spooner 1844–1930
English clergyman

❧ But there, everything has its drawbacks, as the
man said when his mother-in-law died, and
they came down upon him for the funeral
expenses.

Jerome K. Jerome 1859–1927
English writer

❧ Where there's a will, there are relations.

Michael Gill